IHRS
250·260 6798

Stirred by a Noble Theme
God's Heart, Israel and the Nations

Stirred by a Noble Theme
God's Heart, Israel and the Nations

Annie Elliott

Stirred by a Noble Theme
God's Heart, Israel and the Nations

Published by Hodos
480 Vernon Road
Gatineau, Quebec
J9J 3K5
Canada
(819) 778-2681
www.hodos.ca

© Annie Elliott, 2016

Stirred by a Noble Theme: ISBN 978-2-924586-10-5 (print)
Stirred by a Noble Theme: ISBN 978-2-924586-11-2 (digital)

All rights reserved. No part of this publication can be reproduced, stored in a retrieval system or transmitted in any form or by any means – electronic, mechanical, photocopy, recording or otherwise – without prior written permission from the publisher. The only exception would be brief quotations for printed reviews.

All scripture quotations, unless otherwise indicated are taken from the Holy Bible, New King James Version® **(NKJV)** copyright © are trademarks registered in the United States Patent and Trademark Office by Biblica. Inc. Tm. Used by permission of Zondervan. All rights reserved worldwide. www.zondervan.com.

Scripture quotations marked **(NIV)** are taken from the Holy Bible, New International Version®, NIV®. Copyright © 1973, 1978, 1984, 2011 by Biblica, Inc.™ Used by permission of Zondervan. All rights reserved worldwide. www.zondervan.com The "NIV" and "New International Version" are trademarks registered in the United States Patent and Trademark Office by Biblica, Inc.™

Scripture quotations from The Authorized King James Version **(KJV)**. Rights in the Authorized Version in the United Kingdom are vested in the Crown. Reproduced by permission of the Crown's patentee, Cambridge University Press.

Scripture quotations marked **(NLT)** are taken from the Holy Bible, New Living Translation, copyright ©1996, 2004, 2007, 2013 by Tyndale House Foundation. Used by permission of Tyndale House Publishers, Inc., Carol Stream, Illinois 60188. All rights reserved.

Excerpts from The Jerusalem Bible, copyright ©1966 by Darton, Longman & Todd, Ltd. and Doubleday, a division of Bantam Doubleday Dell Publishing Group, Inc. reprinted by permission.

Graphic Design
Eric Pechin ■ HeavenDesign France
www.facebook.com/HeavenDesigngraphique

DEDICATION

This book is dedicated to
my Lord and Saviour, Jesus Christ, Yeshua HaMashiach.

*"Jesus said to him,
'I am the Way, the Truth, and the Life.
No one comes to the Father except through Me.' "*

John 14:6

"My heart has been stirred by a Noble Theme..."

Psalm 45:1 (NIV)

*"For Zion's sake I will not keep silent,
for Jerusalem's sake I will not remain quiet,
till her vindication shines out like the dawn,
her salvation like a blazing torch."*

Isaiah 62:1 (NIV)

TABLE OF CONTENTS

Dedication 7
Table of Contents 9
Acknowledgements 10
Endorsements 12
Foreword 13
Introduction 17
Prologue 23

- 1 ~ I Will Bless Those Who Bless Israel 33
- 2 ~ God's Covenant Land 57
- 3 ~ God's Favorite City 85
- 4 ~ Israel and Bible Prophecy 107
- 5 ~ As You Do To Israel 125
- 6 ~ Israel's Peace Partners 145
- 7 ~ O Israel, We Stand on Guard for Thee 149
- 8 ~ O Canada, We Stand on Guard for Thee 167
- 9 ~ Watchmen Arise 193
- 10 ~ Stirred by a Noble Theme 205

Epilogue 209
About The Book 215

ACKNOWLEDGEMENTS

The writing of this book

Stirred by a Noble Theme: God's Heart, Israel and the Nations

would not have been possible without the God of Israel, His Word and His loving plans for Israel and the nations as clearly portrayed in the Bible.

To God I am eternally grateful and to Him be the glory!

I extend my sincere appreciation to:

Alan Baker, Ambassador (ret'), Advocate

Former ambassador of Israel to Canada, 2004-2008

Former legal counsel of the Israel's Ministry for Foreign Affairs,

Director, Institute for Contemporary Affairs, Jerusalem Center for Public Affairs

for writing the foreword in this book.

Acknowledgements

Special Thanks to:

Alain Caron, Apostolic Leader of Église Le Chemin
and of the Hodos Network, Gatineau, Quebec, Canada.

William Koenig, White House correspondent,
Director of Koenig - World Watch Daily

for your encouragement, prayers and endorsement of this book.

In addition, I am very grateful to my pastor Alain Caron for his incredible support and the untold hours invested in the final reviews and editing.

I am deeply grateful to many friends, clergy and colleagues mentioned below and also those who chose to remain anonymous, for their loving support, encouragement, invaluable assistance, dedication and patience as they laboured over the manuscripts editing, discerning, proof-reading and praying over this work.

Bern and Marion McLaughlan
Ruth Hawn
Susan Brown-Mahon
Deb Wright
Peggy Hirst
Kathy Church
Lisa McLachlan
Mark Coburn
Noga Abarbanel

ENDORSEMENTS

"*Stirred by a Noble Theme*, written by Annie Elliott, is a journey into the heart of the Lord. With a passion to discover what is most precious to the G-d of Israel, she has postured herself like Mary of Bethany to listen to the Master. What she found is the apple of His eye ~ a land and a people at the centre of the affairs of all nations. You will not see the future with the same eyes after you read *Stirred by a Noble Theme*!"

Alain Caron, Apostolic Leader of Église Le Chemin
and of the Hodos Network, Gatineau, Quebec, Canada.

"Annie Elliott has been a tireless worker for Israel in Canada for many years. She has extraordinary insight of the Canadian government's strong support of Israel and the blessing that comes as spoken of in Genesis 12:3."

William Koenig, White House correspondent,
Director of Koenig - World Watch Daily

FOREWORD

At a time when the international community seems to be unjustly and glibly forsaking Israel and the Jewish People;

At a time when the plague of antisemitism has returned and is rife especially in Europe in the form of vicious and murderous incitement and acts directed against Jews and Jewish stores and synagogues, having forgotten the disastrous Holocaust which took the lives of six million Jews only seventy years ago in Europe;

At a time when this very international community, without reason, and driven by an illogical fear of fanatic Islamist violence, is being manipulated into questioning the very legitimacy of Israel, the very right of Israel to exist as a sovereign Jewish state;

At a time when this same international community, out of the same fear of Islamist violence and threats, is re-establishing it's economic and cultural boycott of Israel in an attempt to strangle Israel and its commercial and cultural ties;

At a time when the world arbitrarily and unjustly criticizes and automatically condemns Israel for daring to defend itself from Arab terror imposed upon it, from rockets indiscriminately fired against Israeli population centers, from terrorists seeking to kill Jews by arbitrarily stabbing them, exploding and running them down in the streets of Jerusalem;

At a time when the Arab world is denying the basic right of Jews to pray at the epicenter of the Jewish religion – Zion, – and is engaged in dreadful incitement against Israel and the Jewish People in order to generate violence and hatred;

At a time when even the most democratic and enlightened countries and societies in the world, for fear of Islamic threats and violence, are under pressure from the Islamic world to censure Israel, to restrict trade and to view her as a rogue state;

At a time when even elements within the Christian Church, abused and manipulated by those who seek to influence the Christian world, set out to reconstruct some of the most basic precepts of the relationship between God and mankind, to cast doubt on His relationship with the Jewish People and Israel, and to determine political policies and viewpoints aimed at alienating their flock and harming Israel;

At such a time, this book *Stirred by a Noble Theme: God's Heart, Israel and the Nations* written by Annie Elliott, comes as a breath of fresh air, a reminder and wake-up call, and a warning to all of humanity, to discard the tragically false, misplaced and manipulative trend of hostility and hatred vis-à-vis Israel and the Jewish People. It is a call to return to the very sources that lay at the foundation of humanity and human civilization and that molded the character of mankind and of international civilization.

Annie Elliott, through scholarly research and study, as well as true devotion to faith and the Bible, traces in this impressive book, the prophecies and learnings, from the first days of our civilization and to present day. This important book points to the dominion of God and His commandments regarding His relationship with the Jewish People and Israel as well as with all humanity, and His expectation as to the behavior of nations and peoples vis-à-vis Israel and the Jewish People.

Reading this thorough and scholarly research, one cannot but be in awe and trepidation at the relevance in today's world, of the messages gleaned from the Bible, the warnings – still very relevant and timely – of the Prophets, and the calls of the scriptures.

I trust and hope that leaders of today's world, as well as all serious people of faith, will indeed heed the messages and warnings so articulately collated and presented by Annie Elliott, and will cast aside the misconceptions and false, manipulative influences that drive their beliefs and actions - before it is too late.

Alan Baker, Ambassador (ret'), Advocate

Former ambassador of Israel to Canada, 2004-2008

Former legal counsel of the Israel's Ministry for Foreign Affairs,

Director, Institute for Contemporary Affairs,
Jerusalem Center for Public Affairs

INTRODUCTION

STIRRED BY A NOBLE THEME
GOD'S HEART, ISRAEL AND THE NATIONS

Stirred by a Noble Theme is a compelling and passionate journey into the heart of God. His loving plans and redemptive purposes for Israel and the nations are clearly woven throughout scripture as His *Noble Theme*.

The things that are important, valued and treasured by God, are plainly revealed throughout the Bible from Genesis to Revelation. They cannot be ignored. God's *Noble Theme* demands a noble response. Alignment with His plans and purposes is paramount for individuals, governments and nations of the world.

God chose a certain place for His *Noble Theme* to begin. That place is Israel.

An understanding of what the Bible says about Israel and the nations is imperative.

We are on a profoundly significant and unparalleled prophetic journey at this critical juncture in time. The State of Israel is under existential threat by radical jihadist Islam, from Iranian nuclear threats and ambitions and prevailing global powers. Terror is shaking the nations.

Men's hearts are failing them for fear. Momentous events are raging every day. The world is in chaos. People are in crisis. Nations are in an uproar. God is in control!

Nations and governments are being weighed in the balance. Global leaders take their stand against the God of Israel and His Anointed One. Nations are colliding in opposition to the God of the Bible over their dealings with Israel, God's covenant people and God's covenant land.

Nations craft their road maps and engineer their peace plans but God's road map trumps them all!

The eyes of the world are riveted on Israel. The conflict and campaign of terror in the Middle East are escalating daily. The Bible is expressly clear regarding the affairs of the nation of Israel and the nations of the world. God is actively engaged. His plans and purposes will not be thwarted and the gates of Hell will never prevail!

In the chapters following, discover God's love and redemptive plan for Israel and the nations. Discover what God says about His covenant land and His covenant people. Discover what God says about Jerusalem. Discover which Biblical prophecies and warnings are relevant today.

Why are nations raging over Jerusalem? Does the Bible indicate that there will be consequences for nations pressuring Israel to divide God's covenant land? Will the 'land for peace' plan work? What happens when nations touch the apple of God's eye?

Whether nations acknowledge the Word of God, His commands, His divine imperatives and warnings or not, God's Word still stands true, forever settled in Heaven for all generations in every dispensation of time. God is watching over His Word to fulfill it!

Isaiah 40:8 *"The grass withers, the flower fades, but the Word of our God stands forever."*

Psalm 119:89 *"Forever, O Lord, Your Word is settled in Heaven."*

Psalm 33:11 *"...but Yahweh's own plan stands firm forever, his heart's counsel from age to age."* (Jerusalem Bible)

Jeremiah 1:12 *"... for I am watching to see that my word is fulfilled."* (NIV)

God invites everyone to participate with Him in the unfolding last-day, end-time drama of epic Biblical proportions.

The line has been drawn. On which side will individuals and nations and churches stand at such a time? On which side will you stand?

The plumb line has been dropped. How will individuals and nations align with God's purposes in this hour? How will the church and mainline denominations align at such a time as this? How will you align?

I invite you on a journey, a millennial journey which began in Eden. This journey will take you through the scriptures and inside the passionate heart, plans and purposes of God to gain a Biblical understanding and divine wisdom about the things that stir God's heart regarding His covenant people, His covenant land and the nations of the world.

My sincere prayer is that your heart would be ~ **Stirred by God's Noble Theme!**

GOD'S NOBLE THEME

Before the dawning of creation, God the Father had a dream.
His Sovereign heart was burning with Heaven's *Noble Theme*.
He was longing for a people, to walk closely by His side,
A people He would treasure in whom He would confide.

When the world was first created, God's Master plan began,
He formed the earth, all living things, and then created man.
God walked each day with Adam, His heart He would convey,
In intimate communion, at the cool of every day.
With Eden full and flourishing, the garden was replete,
But of the tree of knowledge, God simply said, *"Don't eat."*

Only this directive, that man must not defy,
God emphatically told Adam, *"Do not eat or you shall die."*
The consequences followed, the day man fell from grace,
And catastrophic suffering befell the human race.

In time, God chose a nation, to advance His *Noble Theme*.
All peoples of the earth could come and He would then redeem.
And so it was through Abram, God's covenant with man.
By faith one could be justified, in God's redemptive plan.

Through Israel the blessings flowed, for God had given much,
His admonition followed, *"They're My people, do not to touch!"*
He gave them land, a place their own, where they would all abide.
Then told His chosen people, *"It's My land, do not divide!"*
Of His beloved City, Jerusalem of gold,
God said, *"Don't move her boundaries or judgements will unfold."*

The nations in defiance, shook their fists in pride.
They didn't heed God's warnings, His commandments they defied.
Coalition armies, aligned and took their stand,
In the age old battle targeting God's people and His land.

The enemies of Israel contrived a hellish scheme,
To destroy God's chosen people and to thwart God's *Noble Theme*.
They partook in evil counsel, in unison confess,
A scheme to take the holy land, to conquer and possess.

God's *Noble Theme* advancing, the conflict raging still,
Amazing grace was poured out, because it was His will.
For God so loved the nations, He gave His only Son,
He died on Mount Moriah, redemption's work was done.

The flames are fanned in fury, in Satan's wicked plan,
To destroy God's Holy people, still targeting God's land.

The conflict never ending, the nations in collusion,
They're honing out a peace plan, yet walking in delusion.
They contradict the scriptures, with their 'two-state resolution',
This road map, is unbiblical, it isn't God's solution!

The nature of this battle, comes as no surprise,
It's an ancient root of hatred coming in disguise.
The core of the conflict, the suffering and pain,
Is in relation to the question over who will rule and reign,
On God's Holy Mountain, the place He set apart,
The only place on earth, God said that He has placed His heart.

No plan of man or strategy, will bring a resolution,
To the conflict in the Middle East, no viable solution!
An anointed and appointed time awaits God's soon release.
The return of Israel's Sar Shalom, Jesus, Prince of Peace.

He's the answer to the conflict that is raging still,
God's Kingdom come, His will be done, upon His Holy Hill.
For on God's Holy Mountain, yes, the Mountain of Moriah.
He'll come again, forever reign, Yeshua, King Messiah.

PROLOGUE

Author's Note: The prologue and epilogue in *Stirred by a Noble Theme* are introductory and concluding prose purposely and precisely placed to frame the message of this book. In keeping with the theme, the prologue and epilogue express, through poetic liberty, the heart, purposes and plans of God for Israel and the nations as gleaned from scriptures in the Bible.

JERUSALEM 845 BC

Jerusalem was astir, yet again. Joel, son of Pethuel, blazed into town on a sweltering summer afternoon. Another oracle of God trumpeted from the righteous lips of this Hebrew prophet. He blew the shofar in Zion. He sounded the alarm on God's holy mountain. [1] He called a holy convocation, a sacred assembly and implored all the inhabitants of the land to turn to the Lord with fasting and weeping, mourning and repentance. [2]

The nation was reeling in the aftermath of the plague of locusts. What the locust swarm left, the great locusts had eaten; what the great locusts left, the young locusts had eaten; what the young locusts left, other locusts had eaten. [3] The fields mourned, the land lamented, the gates of Zion grieved and the new wine and oil languished. What used to look like Eden was now bleak and barren, dismal and foreboding.

The perilous invasion of locust armies advanced in successive waves as God's judgement. ⁴

The people were quick to respond to the Word of the Lord that was proclaimed by the prophet of God. The elders came. Families gathered. Nursing mothers with babes drew near. The bridegroom came out from his chamber and the bride from her canopy. ⁵ The nation came as one, to the House of the Lord and cried out to God. They wept between the portico and the altar. ⁶ The people rent their hearts instead of their garments. ⁷ They prayed, repented and turned from their wicked ways.

Rays of hope pierced through their darkness. The light of salvation dawned on the nation of Israel once again when Joel decreed an imminent restoration of the land and a revival of the people. The land would rejoice again; the threshing floors would be filled with grain; the vats would overflow with new wine and new oil; ⁸ the trees of the fields would clap their hands; the rocks would praise in jubilant chorus; streams in the desert would burst into song; the beasts of the field would leap with joy; gladness and rejoicing would be heard once again in the House of Adonai, the House of the Lord.

Joel released a crowning proclamation that whosoever would call upon the Name of the Lord would be saved, ⁹ for salvation would come out of Zion and the Word of the Lord from Jerusalem! ¹⁰ The promise of God's Spirit would be poured out on all flesh and signs and wonders would be manifest in the heavens and on earth. ¹¹

God opened the treasures of His storehouse. Salvation, blessing and favor cascaded upon the nation He loved.

After these things, another word was proclaimed through this son of Pethuel. It was a warning to the nations, a sobering message! Whether nations believed it or not, whether nations acknowledged the warnings or not, whether they even considered the God of Israel or not, it would still stand forever in the courts of Heaven and the chronicles of Holy Writ as divine decree. God would watch over this Word to perform it! ¹² There would be serious consequences for any nation that would seek to divide God's covenant land and scatter His chosen people. ¹³

Joel's pronouncement echoed Heaven's proclamation. Prophets sent by Adonai Elohim, the God of Israel, uttered the same sombre decrees. Zechariah, Obadiah and Isaiah voiced similar warnings that would render calamitous consequences.

There was a deep anguish in Joel's heart. He stood in the fear of the Lord. He paused. He reflected!. He meditated. He pondered the far reaching implications of it all. With the forward glance of his *'seer'* eyes, Joel gazed through God's prophetic lens, into the future centuries and millennia. He saw nations and governments fall from their zenith of power. He saw kings and kingdoms cease to exist because they dared to touch the *'Apple of God's eye.'* [14] He saw untold horrors and sufferings. He saw indescribable destruction and natural disasters! He saw economic collapse! He saw dreadful catastrophes and ominous calamities! Indeed, he saw nations crumble because they dared to divide God's covenant land and scatter God's covenant people! [13]

Yet, Joel remembered His God, his covenant making, covenant keeping God, the God of Abraham, Isaac and Jacob. He remembered the covenant given to Abram:

> **Genesis 12:1-3** *"The LORD had said to Abram, "Go from your country, your people and your father's household* **to the land** *I will show you. "I will make you into a great nation, and I will bless you; I will make your name great, and you will be a blessing. I will bless those who bless you, and whoever curses you I will curse; and* **all peoples on earth will be blessed through you.***"* (NIV)

This was God's plan! This was God's *Noble Theme!* His greatness and goodness, His manifold and lavish blessings would flow to and through His chosen people, to all peoples on earth! Nations would tremble and stand in awe of the goodness and the greatness of the Lord!

Joel remembered the words God spoke to Moses on Mount Sinai where God Himself described His own nature and character. This was the God he knew.

> **Exodus 34:6,7** *"Then the Lord came down in the cloud and stood there with him and proclaimed His Name, the Lord. And He passed in front of Moses, proclaiming, "The Lord, the Lord, the compassionate and gracious God, slow to anger, abounding in love and faithfulness, maintaining love to thousands, and forgiving wickedness, rebellion and sin."*

Joel remembered God's *treasured possession*, Israel.

> **Deuteronomy 7:6** *"For you are a people holy to the Lord your God. The Lord your God has chosen you out of all the peoples on the face of the earth to be his people, His treasured possession."* (NIV)

God's *Noble Theme* would stand forever and usher in His salvation and redemption to the ends of the earth, through His *treasured possession*, Israel. He would bring to Himself a people that He would call His own.

> **Isaiah 49:6** *"It is too small a thing for you to be my servant to restore the tribes of Jacob and bring back those of Israel I have kept.* **I will also make you a light for the Gentiles that my salvation may reach to the ends of the earth."**

In God's plan, His *Noble Theme*, God would send His Son, Yeshua, to save the world from their sin and sanctify a people unto himself and bestow upon them eternal life. His plan of salvation was to the Jewish people first, then to the Gentiles.

> **Romans 1:16** *"For I am not ashamed of the gospel, because it is the power of God that brings salvation to everyone who believes: first to the Jew, then to the Gentile."* (NIV)

> **John 3:16** *"For God so loved the world that He gave His only begotten Son, that whoever believes in Him should not perish but have everlasting life."*

This everlasting gift of salvation through Messiah would be born out of the people, the nation and the land of Israel. The love of God would flow through His covenant land, through His covenant people to all nations on earth, to all mankind.

A people created in God's image and likeness, walking in the light of His salvation and glory, living forever with Him in His Holy City, the New Jerusalem. [15]

Suddenly, the sobering words of Zechariah came to mind.

Zechariah 2:8,9 *"...for whoever touches you touches the apple of his eye -* ***I will surely raise my hand against them.***"

Zechariah 12:1-3,9 *"A prophecy: The word of the LORD concerning Israel. The LORD, who stretches out the heavens, who lays the foundation of the earth, and who forms the human spirit within a person, declares: "I am going to make Jerusalem a cup that sends all the surrounding peoples reeling. Judah will be besieged as well as Jerusalem. On that day, when all the nations of the earth are gathered against her, I will make Jerusalem an immovable rock for all the nations. All who try to move it will injure themselves...****On that day I will set out to destroy all the nations that attack Jerusalem.***" (NIV)

Joel's pensive thoughts went deeper still. He remembered the words of Isaiah.

Isaiah 34:8 *"For the Lord has a* ***day of vengeance****, a year of retribution,* ***to uphold Zion's cause.***"

Joel knew also that the holy covenant God made with His people included God's land. They were inseparable. Joel pondered further, the land of Beulah, one of the Hebrew names that God gave to Israel. It meant the land is *'married'* to the people. [16]

On this day, Joel stood in Jerusalem and released the warning in alignment with his contemporaries.

> **Joel 3:1-3** *"In those days and at that time, when I restore the fortunes of Judah and Jerusalem, I will gather all nations and bring them down to the Valley of Jehoshaphat. There **I will enter into judgement for what they did to My inheritance, My people Israel, because they scattered my people among the nations and divided up My land. They cast lots for My people.**"*

Joel remembered his God and stood in awe. He stood in silence as the blazing desert sun set on his beloved city and his cherished and chosen people. His thoughts were drawn heavenward and His eyes soon fixed on the God he loved with all his heart, soul and strength.

Joel knew that day, in the aftermath and afterglow of all that transpired in the land, and having stood in the centre of God's heart and will to deliver Heaven's oracles, that Adonai's plans and purposes were incredibly, indescribably, exceedingly, abundantly far greater than he could think or even begin to imagine.

As he stood in the quietness of the setting sun, in the twinkling of an eye, Joel was caught up in a Heavenly vision. He was transported back in time, to eternity past, before the foundations of the world were created. He was swept into the majestic and brilliant Presence of God Almighty. The atmosphere of Heaven was saturated with a singular and penetrating passion. It was a flaming zeal driven by the deepest of longings, burning from the blazing heart of the Author and Creator of Life. His fiery passion and burning love was a deep longing, a yearning to have a people of His own from every nation and language and tongue and tribe who would walk intimately with Him. [17] The colors of God's love would dance in every heart in the light of His glorious Presence. He would have a people that He would call His own. They would be a crown of glory, a royal diadem in His hand.

> **Isaiah 62:3** *"You shall also be a crown of glory in the hand of the Lord, and a royal diadem in the hand of your God."*
>
> **Malachi 3:17** *"They shall be Mine,"* says the Lord of hosts, *"On the day that I make them **My jewels, My special treasure.**"*

They would be a people adorned in His eternal beauty who could and would know His blessings and His ways, His hand and His heart. They would be a people with whom God would share the secrets of His heart. [18] They would be a people on whom God would lavish every good and perfect gift.[19] He would give them an eternal inheritance that would never fade or perish. They would share His heart, His home and His throne forever! [20]

Yes, God had a plan, a *Noble Theme*, for a people whom He would make in His own image and likeness and woo them unto Himself. He would draw them with cords of love. [21] Everyone was welcome. The Father's heart and arms were extended, even before the dawn of creation. All could have a place inside His noble and righteous heart. Joel saw desire engraved on the face of his God. It was Adonai's magnificent obsession. God's fiery heart was ablaze and pounded with what was about to explode into the greatest drama ever. Conceived in Heaven, the world would be its stage ~ Israel its birthplace. God's dream, His *Noble Theme*, was about to be spoken into existence by His eternal living Words. Joel sensed that no eye could ever fully see, no ear could ever fully hear, no heart could ever fully comprehend [22] all that stirred in the heart of God.

This would be God's indescribable gift to mankind. This was Heaven's *Noble Theme* and the glory of God.

> **Psalm 19:1-6** *"The heavens declare the glory of God; and the firmament shows His handiwork. Day unto day utters speech, and night unto night reveals knowledge. There is no speech nor language where their voice is not heard. Their line has gone out through all the earth, and their words to the end of the world."*

Mingled with God's holy and righteous zeal for a people, Joel saw a burning jealousy in the heart of God for a *'certain place.'*

> **Zechariah 8:2** *"This is what the Almighty says: I am very jealous for Zion; I am burning with jealousy for her."*

The *'certain place'* would one day be called God's favorite place, the place of His throne, the place of His heart. It was a place that God would create and make for Himself.

> **Exodus 15:17** *"You will bring them in and plant them in the **mountain of Your inheritance**, in the place, O Lord, which **You have made for Your own dwelling**, the sanctuary, O Lord, which **Your hands have established.**"*

The place would one day be called Jerusalem, in the land that would one day be called Israel. A place where God's chief joy and singular passion would be consummated. Every emotion poured out of the sovereign heart of God penetrating the depths of Joel's being. It consumed him, immortality touching mortality. God's heart touching man. Heaven was about to invade earth.

Joel stood speechless, in reverence, awe and wonder. The *Noble Theme* of Heaven resonated in the chambers of eternity-past. It was the refrain of God.

> *No greater joy could ever be known,*
> *Than to walk with a people and call them My own.*
> *No greater delight could I ever conceive,*
> *Than a people to whom only Me they would cleave.*
> *I'll give them My heart and I'll give them My hand,*
> *My Covenant People, I'll give them My land.*
> *I'll give them My Word, to embrace and possess.*
> *Through My Chosen People, all nations I'll bless.*
> *My Son I will send, to save them from sin.*
> *When they trust Him as Saviour, He will come in.*
> *No greater joy, than to walk by my side,*
> *A people, My own, in whom I call bride.*
> *With Me forever, this is My dream,*
> *Heaven's song of Redemption, My Noble Theme!*

Through the backward glance of the prophet's lens, Joel saw from eternity past, that the consuming fire of God's burning heart was about to ignite in the dimension of time and space. The imminent drama was about to unfold. The first act was about to commence. The Genesis of God's Master plan was standing at the threshold of time. Joel stood speechless and overwhelmed. His eyes were transfixed and his heart was captivated and completely ~ ***Stirred by God's Noble Theme!***

Scriptural References:

1) Joel 2:1
2) Joel 1:14
3) Joel 1:4
4) Joel 1,2
5) Joel 2:16
6) Joel 2:17
7) Joel 2:13
8) Joel 2:24
9) Joel 2:32
10) Isaiah 2:3
11) Joel 2:28,29
12) Jeremiah 1:12
13) Joel 3:2
14) Zechariah 2:8,9
15) Revelation 21:2
16) Isaiah 62:4
17) Revelation 7:9
18) Deuteronomy 29:29
19) James 1:17
20) Revelation 3:21
21) Hosea 11:4; Jeremiah 31:3
22) Isaiah 64:4; 1 Corinthians 2:9

CHAPTER ONE

I WILL BLESS THOSE WHO BLESS ISRAEL

Genesis 12:1-3 *"The LORD had said to Abram, Go from your country, your people and your father's household **to the land** I will show you. I will make you into a great nation, and I will bless you; I will make your name great, and you will be a blessing. I will bless those who bless you, and whoever curses you I will curse; and **all peoples on earth will be blessed through you.**"* (NIV)

The Abrahamic covenant is simple, yet profoundly far-reaching. It is vast in scope, embracing not only Israel but all peoples of the earth and all generations. It begins with a Sovereign God and a chosen people through whom He would bless all the families of nations. All that God pledged and promised to His covenant people Israel was extended to all people. This is God's good news! This is God's *Noble Theme!*

God loves the people of Israel with an everlasting love.

Jeremiah 31:3 *"Long ago the LORD said to Israel: I have loved you, my people, with an everlasting love. With unfailing love I have drawn you to myself."* (NLT)

God equally loves the nations of the world.

John 3:16 *"**For God so loved the world** that He gave His only begotten Son, that whoever believes in Him should not perish but have everlasting life."*

God's redemptive plan for the entire world is the good news of the gospel of Jesus Christ ~ for all mankind!

Consider Galatians 3:8. God preached the good news of the gospel to Abraham first when He spoke to him and called him out of his country.

> **Galatians 3:8** *"And the scripture, foreseeing that God would justify the Gentiles by faith,* **preached the gospel to Abraham** *beforehand, saying,* **"In you all the nations shall be blessed."**

When the Apostle Paul spoke these words to the Galatians, he was quoting from Genesis 12:3, the Abrahamic covenant. You might ask, *"How can that be? The gospel preached beforehand? Did Abraham know about Yeshua (Jesus' name in Hebrew) thousands of years before He appeared on earth?"* Jesus made an amazing statement, speaking to the Jewish people thousands of years after the time of Abraham:

> **John 8:56** *"Your father Abraham rejoiced to see* **My** *day, and he saw it and was glad."*

What did Abraham see? Whom did Abraham see? The Bible does not say exactly how the gospel was preached to Abraham or what exactly Abraham saw, but this we know, God preached the gospel to Abraham! That is awesome! Wouldn't you have loved to hear that sermon?

God has woven His heart, His *Noble Theme*, the good news of the gospel of Jesus Christ, Yeshua Messiah, as a golden thread throughout the scriptures from Genesis, right up to the very last chapter of the Bible. Abraham saw by faith. He was looking for *'the City'* whose Builder and Maker and Architect was God.

> **Hebrews 11:10** *"....for he waited for the city which has foundations, whose builder and maker is God."*

The prophetic foreshadowing of Messiah is evident in every book of the Old Testament. Thousands of years have transpired and pages of history are still being written, awaiting the triumphal, glorious climax and conclusion that will mark the beginning of *'forever.'* The new heavens, the new earth, the new Jerusalem will come down from heaven with the crowning majestic reign of Yeshua Messiah, the Lamb of God, as John the Baptist said, *"...Who takes away the sin of the world."* God's glorious and *Noble Theme* is His plan of salvation for Israel and mankind. Indeed, the glorious good news of the gospel was preached to Abram and essentially found in the Abrahamic covenant.

> **Genesis 12:1-3** *"The LORD had said to Abram, Go from your country, your people and your father's household **to the land** I will show you. I will make you into a great nation, and I will bless you; I will make your name great, and you will be a blessing. **I will bless those who bless you, and whoever curses you I will curse; and all peoples on earth will be blessed through you.**"* (NIV)

THOSE WHO BLESS ISRAEL

God states clearly that those who bless Israel, He would bless! The implicit and explicit purposes of His heart have always been to bless all nations of the earth through a chosen people, Israel.

God's promises to Israel and the nations stand firm forever! As Bible believing evangelical Christians, we embrace the Word of God and view the Bible as God's book of instruction and wisdom.

> **2 Timothy 3:16** *"All Scripture is given by inspiration of God, and is profitable for doctrine, for reproof, for correction, for instruction in righteousness,"*

The Bible reveals the heart, mind and plans of God for all mankind.

> **Psalm 33:11** *"But the plans of the LORD stand firm forever, the purposes of his heart through all generations."* (NIV)

The doctrines in the Bible are holy, its precepts are true and its history accurate.

The Bible is our road map in life and our guiding moral compass.

God loves Israel! As Christians, we are called to love Israel. It's a Biblical imperative. It simply is incomprehensible that one could be a Christian and not love, pray for and bless the Jewish people.

We choose to love what and whom God loves and hate what God hates. With respect to the Jewish people and the nation of Israel, the scriptures speak unmistakably of God's everlasting love and plans for Israel and the Jewish people as His *treasured possession*.

> **Deuteronomy 7:6** *"For you are a people holy to the Lord your God. The Lord your God has chosen you out of all the peoples on the face of the earth to be His people, **His treasured possession.**"* (NIV)

> **Deuteronomy 26:16-19** *"The LORD your God commands you this day to follow these decrees and laws; carefully observe them with all your heart and with all your soul. You have declared this day that the LORD is your God and that you will walk in obedience to him, that you will keep his decrees, commands and laws ~ that you will listen to him. And the LORD has declared this day that you are his people, **His treasured possession** as he promised, and that you are to keep all his commands. He has declared that he will set you in praise, fame and honor high above all the nations he has made and that you will be a people holy to the LORD your God, as he promised."* (NIV)

The Hebrew word for *'treasured possession'* is *'cegullah.'* (Strong's Concordance 5459) Six times in scripture this word is used to describe Israel as God's special, treasured or *'peculiar'* possession. From the Greek language the word is *'peculium'* as in a king's private property or exclusive possession for his own private use. The King's peculiar treasure, his *'peculium'* was locked up, guarded, treasured and set aside for His noble purposes. Israel was set aside as God's treasured possession. Jewish Rabbis have commented that God's treasured possession was set apart for relationship with God alone and no other thus the treasured possession of a loving and jealous God.

Zechariah 1:14 *"Then the angel who was speaking to me said, Proclaim this word: This is what the Lord Almighty says:* **I am very jealous for Jerusalem and Zion***"* (NIV)

Zechariah 8:2 *"This is what the Lord Almighty says:* **I am very jealous for Zion; I am burning with jealousy for her.***"* (NIV)

In Exodus 19, God expressed His love to the Jewish people by stating that He carried them out of Egypt on eagles' wings and brought them to Himself. He clearly stated that Israel was His treasured possession. Jewish commentators say that the exchange and the response of the elders and the people was like a marriage proposal or a binding covenant. The people responded in unison.

Exodus 19:8 *"The people all responded together,* **"We will do everything the LORD has said."** *So Moses brought their answer back to the LORD."*

Jewish sages state that this was the beginning of the nation of Israel. The entire community stood with one voice and proclaimed their response to Adonai's invitation.

Several times in scripture God likens His relationship with the people of Israel as a marriage which He initiated between Himself and his people, whether the bride mentioned was Israel, Jacob, Judah, and Jerusalem.

Isaiah 54:5 *"For your Maker is your husband ~ the LORD Almighty is his name!"* (NIV)

Isaiah 62:5 *"...as a bridegroom rejoices over his bride, so will your God rejoice over you."* (NIV)

In the book of Jeremiah God refers to Himself as Israel's husband.

Jeremiah 31:32,37 *"It will not be like the covenant I made with their ancestors when I took them by the hand to lead them out of Egypt, because they broke my covenant,* **though I was a husband to them,***" declares the LORD. This is what the LORD says:*

> "Only if the heavens above can be measured and the foundations of the earth below be searched out will I reject all the descendants of Israel because of all they have done," declares the LORD."

As Christians, by the grace of God, we are called to bless, love, serve, comfort, pray for and support Israel and the Jewish people. There is a distinct Biblical mandate to bless Israel!

The Abrahamic covenant is foundational and the best place from which to begin.

> **Genesis 12:3** *"I will bless those who bless you, and I will curse him who curses you: and in you all the families of the earth shall be blessed."*

A deeper and fuller understanding of what God is both saying and implying can be gleaned if we look at the Hebrew meanings of some of the words in this verse.

The Hebrew word for *'bless'* is *'barak'* (Strong's 1288) which literally means *'to kneel.'* The implication here is to take the posture of heart by kneeling before someone to honor, to respect, to salute, to prefer, to defer, to serve, to bless and even lay down one's life. The true expression of blessing Israel goes far beyond lip service. To bless Israel is to back one's words with supportive and loving action.

When God states that He would *'bless'* those who bless Israel, the same Hebrew word is used, *'barak,'* meaning *'to kneel.'* This scripture ought to arrest the reader. Could it be that Almighty God, the God of the universe, would kneel before those who bless Israel? What does this imply? Let us ponder this. Could it be that the word picture here portrays God kneeling, as a father kneels before his small son? The father meets the small son at his level to engage his heart and enrich his life. This is a picture of sweet and intimate communion ~ eye to eye, heart to heart. There would be a face to face encounter that would be far more impacting than a father towering over his son and speaking down to him. God would bless and lift up His countenance upon those who bless Israel. Could this be the picture that this verse is painting? God will spiritually enrich the lives of those who bless Israel. God would lavish upon those who bless Israel manifold blessings from His hand and heart.

Conversely, the second half of the verse invokes a curse for those who curse or oppose the nation and people of Israel.

The Hebrew language is much more comprehensive than the English language. In Genesis 12:3, the original Hebrew text uses two different words for the English word *'curse.'* The two Hebrew words are: *'qalal'* (Strong's 7043) and *'arar.'* (Strong's 779)

> **Genesis 12:3** *"I will bless those who bless you, and I will curse (arar) him who curses (qalal) you: and in you all the families of the earth shall be blessed."*

One may think that to curse Israel is to be outwardly, openly and aggressively anti-Semitic. Indeed, it does mean this but there is more to this word than meets the English eye. Where the English word *'curse'* is translated from the Hebrew word *'qalal,'* the primary root meaning is: to make light of, to lightly esteem, to be indifferent, to make insignificant, to distance yourself emotionally and physically, to belittle, to despise, to afflict. Wow! That says a whole lot more in Hebrew than it does in English. Could it be that God is speaking to Abram and saying that any nation or individual that is indifferent or lightly esteems Israel falls onto the side of cursing Israel? There is no middle or neutral ground. There is no sitting on the fence with respect to Israel. We are either on the side of actively blessing or actively/indifferently cursing!

With respect to the second use of the English word *'curse'* in the Abrahamic covenant, the Hebrew word is *'arar.'* The primary root meaning of this word means to bitterly curse, to put under a curse, to denounce as evil, to detest and to withhold a blessing, a solemn utterance intended to invoke a supernatural power to inflict harm or punishment on someone or something. Could it be that to be indifferent towards Israel and the Jewish people, is to fall on the side of cursing Israel? At the very least, the person who is indifferent towards Israel would fall short of receiving the fullness of the blessings that otherwise might be theirs.

It is important to mention that though there is a promise of receiving blessing when one blesses Israel, the motive for loving and serving and blessing Israel and the Jewish people should not be self-serving or self-seeking. The motive should be purely on the basis of loving the people whom God loves and esteems as *'the apple of His eye.'*

God has plans and purposes for individuals and nations of the world. It is His desire that peoples and nations would cooperate with His glorious and noble plans and choose to bless Israel and align with His heart and purposes for Israel as the Bible clearly states.

The nations that have cursed the Jewish people have experienced the curse of God.

> **Zechariah 2:8,9** *"For this is what the LORD Almighty says... for **whoever touches you (Israel) touches the apple of His eye - I will surely raise my hand against them...**"* (NIV)

The Bible is replete with examples of the blessings and curses on individuals or nations that either blessed or cursed Israel. Also, history has proven beyond reasonable doubt that the nations that have blessed the Jewish people have experienced the blessing and favor of God. The contrary is also true. Those who have cursed Israel have invoked the judgment and curse of God upon themselves.

In an article fund on the *Why Israel* website, *'The Law of Blessing and Curse,'* this is evident.

> ***Blessing and Curse in the Bible*** *"There are many examples of this law put into practice in the Bible. Here are just a few:*
>
> • *The Pharaoh of Egypt repressed the Jews and refused to let them go. His empire was destroyed and he was drowned in the Red Sea together with his army.*
>
> • *The Assyrian and Babylonian empires destroyed Israel and as a result were diminished. The Bible says: 'Therefore this is what the Lord Almighty, God of Israel, says: "I will punish the king of Babylon and his land as I punished the king of Assyria'* *(Jeremiah 50:18). In 586 B.C. the Babylonians ravaged the*

temple in Jerusalem. After that the Medes devastated Babel. The prophet says the following about that: 'The Lord will take vengeance, vengeance for his temple' (Jeremiah 51:11 NIV). Besides examples of curses, there are also examples of blessing.

- Moses' father-in-law was a priest of a heathen nomad tribe called the Kenites. They supported Israel and were blessed for generations. A part of that tribe was even included into Israel.

- In Canaan there was a city that found a sneaky way to make peace with Joshua's army. That city, Gibeon, was spared when God's wrath poured over that godless region. Throughout history following these biblical examples, we will name just a few of the dozens of examples from 'regular' history that illustrate the law of blessing and curse:

- Charles the Great (768-814) stood up for the persecuted Jews. In spite of warnings from the Roman Catholic Church, he appointed them into high positions in trade and in the government. He and his countries were blessed. He brought order, peace and justice to his large empire and had his subjects educated. Unfortunately, his son Louis the Pious discontinued such politics and before long things started to get worse.

- In the beginning of the 5th century, the Jews in Spain were doing well and therefore, so was Spain. Two centuries later horrendous persecution started and so judgement followed. In 711 the Muslims of North Africa walked right over Spain.

- When the Jews were exiled from Spain and Portugal at the end of the 15th century, many of them found a safe haven in Turkey. At that time Turkey left its primitive past behind it and developed into a world empire. The sultan knew what he was doing. He noted that it was foolish of the king of Spain to chase out the Jews, because it would turn out to be a blessing for Turkey.

- In 1580 Amsterdam lovingly took persecuted Jews in and it soon became a large powerful city. The Jews even called Amsterdam the Jerusalem of the West. Unfortunately, not much of that remains nowadays.

Today: *Let's just look at England and the United States. In the second half of the 13th century, the Jews in England suffered severe persecution and were even banned from England in 1290. It was not until 1657 that the Protestant leader of England, Oliver Cromwell, allowed the Jews to return. England immediately prospered as a nation. The pro-Jewish politics were set forth by the Dutch Stadtholder William III, who then became king of England. England then grew to one of the most powerful kingdoms the world has ever known. At the height of its power, in 1917, England gave the Jews the right to return to the Promised Land, which at that time was called Palestine. That right was later officially recognized by the League of Nations and the United Nations.*

However, a few years later, England betrayed the Jews by choosing sides with the hostile Arabs. As a result, England went downhill fast and in 1956 the British prime minister signed "over to you" to the president of the United States. Since then the United States has become the most powerful country in the world. To a certain extent they have defended tiny Israel from the rage of the surrounding Arab countries. But the U.S. has received many warnings from above. A researcher discovered more than twenty cases in which a disaster in the United States coincided with American pressure on Israel to give land to the Arabs. "I will bless those that bless you and curse those that curse you" is a historical pattern that continues today.

The anti-Israel sentiment in the world does not predict good things! The rising anti-Semitism could just be the last drop when it comes to God's anger about all the injustice and sin in the world.

(http://www.whyisrael.org/2010/07/26/the-law-of-blessing-and-curse/)

HAS EUROPE BEEN CURSED?

The following article written by Zalmi Unsdorfer was posted on the *Israel News* website on September 17th, 2015.

"The hordes of migrants overrunning European borders has reached epic, almost biblical proportions and shows no sign of stopping. It is as if one continent is being decanted into another; a Third World poured into the First World.

Ironically most of these migrants have made their first landfall on the islands of Greece which so recently caused Europe's greatest financial crisis and whose bailout has turned the Euro into confetti money. I am thinking: why this and why now?

As a religious person I see divine intervention in all things and have learned that the G-d of Israel seeks His vengeance Middah K'Neged Middah. This principle was used to drown Pharaoh Ramses and his charioteers as the lex talionis for ordering the drowning of every Jewish firstborn. There are many other examples throughout scripture and our very laws are built on proportional punishment, right down to the eye-for-an-eye.

Another divine principle is ואברכה מברכיך ומקללך אאר – *that G-d will bless those who bless our people and will curse those who curse us.*

The EU has been at the forefront of anti-Israel activism, supporting declarations of unilateral Palestinian statehood on sovereign Jewish land. Europe's academia and trades unions are unashamed patrons of the world BDS (Boycotts, Divestments, Sanctions) movement. Their aims are twofold. To delegitimize Israel as a sovereign Jewish state and to destroy her economy with sanctions and discriminatory labelling of her exports.

How does the God of the Exodus judge a nation that denies the legitimacy of His people's borders? Answer: He makes a mockery of their own borders.

How does the God of the Exodus judge a nation that seeks to destroy the economy of His people's state? Answer: He makes a mockery of their own money.

That's my answer to "why this and why now?" Middah K'Neged Middah.

Last year, at the height of his polling lead to win the UK general election, Jewish opposition leader Ed Milliband demanded that his Labour Party MPs must support a parliamentary vote to recognize 'Palestine' as an independent state. Against all predictions he lost the subsequent general election in a major upset. If that wasn't enough, he has now been replaced by a Marxist oddball who is tipped to keep Labour out of power for a generation.

Is it a coincidence that the Labour party which was so anxious to recognise the PLO as a state now has a leader who doesn't accept the legitimacy of the English queen?

If, on the eve of that Palestine debate with Milliband on sure course to win the election, you would have presented this scenario as a crystal ball to Labour Party members they'd have laughed at you.

But He who laughs last is usually looking after the Jewish people.

As I write these lines, EU states are scrambling all over themselves for the most sought-after commodity ... razor wire fencing. How rich that these are the same people who excoriated the Jews for building a security fence which stopped 95 percent of terror attacks on our people.

May He laugh the longest."

(http://www.israelnationalnews.com/Blogs/Message.aspx/7495#.Vfp08t9VhBc)

YOUR PEOPLE WILL BE MY PEOPLE

The story of Ruth is an outstanding example of one who blesses Israel and subsequently steps into the amazing blessings and favor of God. Ruth, a Moabite Gentile, clung to her Jewish mother-in-law, Naomi, and made a pledge that changed her life. Her pledge and loving actions even contributed to shaping Biblical history with respect to the lineage of Messiah.

> **Ruth 1:16-17** *"But Ruth replied, 'Don't urge me to leave you or turn back from you. Where you go I will go, and where you stay, I will stay. Your people will be my people and your God my God. Where you die, I will die, and there I will be buried. May the Lord deal with me be it ever so severely, if anything but death separates you and me."* (NIV)

Ruth's pledge of love, her demonstrated commitment and dedication to Naomi, her Jewish mother-in-law, is a beautiful illustration of one who walked in the Abrahamic covenant blessing of... *"those who bless Israel, God would bless."*

After the death of Naomi's husband Elimelech and her two sons, Mahlon and Kilion, Naomi heard that the famine was over and there was bread in the land of Judah once again. She made plans to return to Bethlehem, her home. Interestingly enough, the name Bethlehem in Hebrew means, House of Bread: *'beit'* (Strong's 1004) means *'house'* and *'lechem'* (Strong's 3899) means *'bread'*.

One of the most significant and noteworthy parts of the story of Ruth is when Naomi told her two Gentile daughters-in-law to return to their mothers' homes and prayed that God would grant that each find rest in the home of another husband. At first, both Ruth and Orpah expressed their desire to stay with Naomi. Upon Naomi's insistence to return, the responses of Orpah and Ruth were strikingly different.

> **Ruth 1:14** *"At this they wept aloud again. Then Orpah kissed her mother-in-law goodbye, but Ruth clung to her."* (NIV)

Many Christian Bible commentators have stated that the story of Ruth can be interpreted as two different responses demonstrated toward Israel. Today, many mainline churches and denominations, like Orpah, have turned their backs on Israel and preach replacement theology. Many have implemented boycotts, divestments and sanctions against Israel. They like Orpah, have turned their backs and have kissed Israel goodbye.

On the other hand, a growing number of individuals and church denominations, like Ruth, are actively and lovingly supporting and blessing Israel.

Orpah kissed Naomi her Jewish mother-in-law goodbye. It is of interest to note that nothing is ever mentioned of Orpah again after she turned her back on Naomi. Interestingly, the name Orpah (Strong's 6203, 6204) means: the back of the neck, skull, mane, stiff necked. Orpah walked away! The last thing Naomi saw was the back of Orpah's head. This is a prophetic picture of turning one's back on Israel ~ a walking away, a separation, standing aloof and distancing oneself from Israel.

Not so with Ruth (Strong's 7327). Her name means: friendship, mate, neighbor. Ruth clung to Naomi. Nothing would dissuade her. She said, *"Your people shall be my people"*. This is a beautiful picture of what our response as Christian Gentiles should be toward Israel. The Hebrew word for *'cling'* is *'dabaq'* (Strong's 1692) which means: to cleave, to cling for life, to adhere, to be joined together, to fasten its grip, to be steadfast.

As the story unfolds, Ruth steps into a succession of divine appointments, incredible favor and the manifold blessing of God.

Ruth and Naomi make their way to Bethlehem. As God's providential orchestration would have it, Ruth ended up gleaning in the fields of Boaz, who happened to be a man of standing and also happened to be a kinsmen redeemer of the clan of Elimelech, Ruth's father-in-law. Boaz, happened to go into his fields to greet his harvesters on the very day that Ruth happened to be gleaning. His eyes happened to fall upon Ruth and as the providential hand of God orchestrated the succession of events, they married. As it turned out, they had a son,

Obed, the father of Jesse, the Father of King David. Ruth stepped into her destiny and was sovereignly woven into the lineage of Jesus Christ, Messiah, Son of David. A succession of *'happenstances'* was sovereignly ordained by the hand of God and set into place the day Ruth clung to Naomi, the day she chose to bless Israel.

The Hebrew word for *'as it turned out'* is *'miqreh'* (Strong's 4745) which means by happenstance, good fortune, divinely orchestrated. The King James translation states:

> **Ruth 2:3** *"And she went, and came, and gleaned in the field after the reapers: and **her hap was to light on** a part of the field belonging unto Boaz, who was of the kindred of Elimelech."* (KJV)

It was none other than the hand of God divinely orchestrating the events and happenings in Ruth's life. She was supernaturally lead to land in the field of her kinsman-redeemer, Boaz.

It was Ruth's *'hap'* to light upon the field of Boaz. I believe this is a demonstration of the invisible hand of God, ordering Ruth's footsteps because she selflessly chose to cling to, serve and bless Israel.

With Ruth as an example of blessing Israel, would it not stand to reason that those who choose to bless Israel would also experience a succession of *'miqreh'* moments or events orchestrated by the One who promised to bless those who bless Israel?

On a personal note, my life was forever changed on a Sunday morning in May, 1999 when I first heard this message preached about the story of Ruth, as it related to standing with and blessing Israel. The lights went on for me. I believe it was my *'hap'* to light upon a certain congregation to hear that particular preacher deliver a passionate message that would so profoundly change my life. I knew I would never be the same. In my heart, I made a Ruth-like pledge, *"Your people shall be my people!"* What a joy it has been in my journey to find that it was my *'hap'* to light upon a succession of circumstances, so ordained by the hand of God that would propel me forward in my personal journey *For Zion's Sake.*

STANDING ALOOF

The book of Obadiah stands as an ensign. It is a sobering warning of God's impending judgment against a people who distanced themselves both physically and emotionally from Israel during her time of need.

Obadiah 11 *"On the day you stood aloof..."* (NIV)

While Jerusalem was in desperate need of allies, while foreigners entered her gates, while strangers carried off her wealth, the Edomites *'stood aloof.'* In verse 11, Obadiah states that while the Edomites *'stood aloof,'* at a distance and watched the plight of Jerusalem and did nothing, God said that they were *'just like one of them!'* That is a sobering statement! The implication is, to stand by and watch the plight of their distant cousins, their Jewish brethren, and not come to their aid, was as bad as perpetrating and executing the offenses against them. Standing aloof invoked the judgment of God! To stand idly by and do nothing was as ruth-less (no pun intended) as the perpetrators of the evil and violence. *"You were just like one of them!"* This has far reaching implications even today! The nations are being weighed in the balance according to the Word of God. Their stand and how they align with Israel is the qualifying or disqualifying factor.

The Hebrew word *'to stand aloof'* is *'neqed'* (Strong's 5048) which means to stand on the other side, to remove yourself and distance yourself physically and emotionally, to be complacent, to care less about something, opposite to. The meaning and implications are similar to *'qalal,'* the Hebrew word *'to curse.'*

AS YOU DO TO ISRAEL

Obadiah 15 *"As you have done, it will be done to you; your deeds will return upon your own head."* (NIV)

God has set precise universal laws in place. One of them is the law of sowing and reaping. The Abrahamic covenant is reflective of this law of seed bearing fruit after its own kind.

Genesis 12:3 *"I will bless those who bless you, and I will curse him who curses you."*

Throughout the Bible, the principles of the law of sowing and reaping continue to be upheld.

Galatians 6:7 *"Do not be deceived, God is not mocked; for whatever a man sows, that he will also reap."*

Psalm 7:16 *"His trouble shall return upon his own head, and his violent dealing shall come down on his own crown."*

It stands to reason that individuals or nations that are indifferent toward Israel, who aggressively or passively stand against Israel or those who stand in violation to God's Word regarding the land and the people of Israel would invoke the curse or judgement of God upon themselves. As a person or nation does to Israel, so God would do to them ~ in like measure!

JUDGING THE NATIONS

Matthew 25:31-33 *"When the Son of Man comes in His glory, and all the holy angels with Him, then He will sit on the throne of His glory. **All the nations will be gathered before Him**, and He will separate them one from another, as a shepherd divides his sheep from the goats. And He will set the sheep on His right hand, but the goats on the left."*

When Jesus returns, as King of kings and Lord of lords, and gathers all nations before Him, He will make a distinction between the sheep and goat nations. The measure by which nations are judged will be weighed by their participation in God's redemptive purposes in the earth with respect to their treatment of the Jewish people.

Matthew 25:34-40 *"Then the King will say to those on His right hand, 'Come, you blessed of My Father, inherit the kingdom prepared for you from the foundation of the world: for I was hungry and you gave Me food; I was thirsty and you gave Me drink; I was a stranger and you took Me in; I was naked* *and you clothed Me; I was sick and you visited Me; I was in prison and you came to Me.'* (NIV)

*"Then the righteous will answer Him, saying, 'Lord, when did we see You hungry and feed You, or thirsty and give You drink? When did we see You a stranger and take You in, or naked and clothe You? Or when did we see You sick, or in prison, and come to You?' And the King will answer and say to them, 'Assuredly, I say to you, **inasmuch as you did it to one of the least of these My brethren, you did it to Me.**'"* (NIV)

Jesus' response will be very clear! *"I tell you the truth, whatever you did for the least of these brothers of mine, you did it for Me."*

Jesus was speaking of his brothers, His flesh and blood brothers, the Jewish people! The literal translation of the word *'brothers'* means those born of the same womb, flesh and blood ~ the Jewish People! Nations will be judged based on their treatment of the Jewish people!

ISRAEL, THE FOREMOST OF THE NATIONS

In another portion of scripture we see again, a glimpse into the divine connection between Israel and the nations.

When God speaks of Israel and the nations, He clearly mentions Israel as the foremost and chief among the nations. God has sovereignly ordained and established Israel as the leading nation through whom all nations of the earth will be blessed. The nations would fare well to recognize this.

Jeremiah 31:7 *"For thus says the Lord: 'Sing with gladness for Jacob, and shout among **the chief of the nations**; Proclaim, give praise, and say, 'O Lord, save Your people, the remnant of Israel!'"*

FOR ZION'S SAKE

Isaiah 62:1 *"For Zion's sake I will not keep silent, for Jerusalem's sake I will not remain quiet, till her vindication shines out like the dawn, her salvation like a blazing torch."* (NIV)

Isaiah 62:6, 7 *"I have posted watchmen on your walls, Jerusalem; they will never be silent day or night. You who call on the LORD, give yourselves no rest, and give him no rest till he establishes Jerusalem and makes her the praise of the earth."* (NIV)

The watchmen who call on the Name of the Lord and stand with Israel in steadfast determination will be found faithful in prayer until Jerusalem will surely be established as *'the'* praise in all the earth!

COMFORT MY PEOPLE

Isaiah 40:1,2 *"**Comfort, yes, comfort My people!** says your God. Speak comfort to Jerusalem."*

This prophetic directive to comfort God's people was primarily written to the Jewish prophets and the people of Israel but can be applied to foreigners and strangers, those outside the commonwealth of Israel.

Throughout history, the Jewish people have endured untold hardship, suffering and persecution. The brutal horrors of the Holocaust, the pogroms, the crusades and the Inquisition have left their indelible marks and deep-seated scars on the souls of the Jewish people.

There is a rising tide of global anti-Semitism targeting the Jewish people today. Isaiah's exhortation to *"Comfort, yes, comfort My people"* is a moral imperative, a high and holy calling wherever and whenever possible, to speak tenderly to the heart of God's chosen people. There isn't a Jewish person I know who has not felt the stinging barbs and poisonous arrows of anti-Semitism. Isaiah's entreaty to comfort God's people is tragically and increasingly needed in the face of today's rising tide of global anti-Semitism.

Anti-Zionism and anti-Semitism are dangerously similar. Anti-Zionism, masked in legitimate criticism of Israel, in most cases is basically a new terminology or expression of an age-old hatred of the Jewish people.

I WILL BECKON TO THE GENTILES

Isaiah 49:22 *"Thus says the Lord God: Behold, I will lift My hand in an oath to the nations, and set up My standard for the peoples; **They shall bring your sons in their arms, and your daughters shall be carried on their shoulders;"***

God is bringing His people back to their covenant land, the land of Israel. After two thousand years in the Diaspora, millions of Jewish people have returned and made *'aliyah.'* Aliyah means to ascend. It is the emigration of the Jewish people from the Diaspora back to the land of Israel. The restoration of Israel and the return of His people are profoundly significant! This is amazing evidence of God's faithfulness to His Word in the fulfilling of hundreds of prophecies concerning the return of the Jewish People to their ancient homeland. In Tom Hess' book, *'Let My People Go,'* he lists 700 verses of scripture where God promises the Land of Canaan to His chosen people and commands or encourages them to return to the Land of Israel which He gave to them as an everlasting inheritance. These scriptures are found in Appendix 'A' at the end of his book. Page 121.

(http://jeremiah111.org/wp-content/uploads/2012/04/BOOK-let-my-people-go.pdf)

There is an invitation, a Biblical mandate, through the prophet Isaiah, to partner with God in helping bring the Jewish people back home.

Isaiah 49:22 *"Behold, I will lift My hand in an oath to the nations, and set up My standard for the peoples; **They shall bring your sons in their arms, And your daughters shall be carried on their shoulders"***

Christians have an awesome opportunity to participate with God in the great end time enterprise of *'aliyah.'*

> **Amos 9:14,15** *"I will bring back the captives of My people Israel; they shall build the waste cities and inhabit them; They shall plant vineyards and drink wine from them; They shall also make gardens and eat fruit from them.* ***I will plant them in their land, and no longer shall they be pulled up from the land I have given them,*** *" says the Lord your God."*

Israel's population reached 8,412,000 on the eve of the Jewish year 5776, (2015) the Central Bureau of Statistics reported. The stats bureau forecasts that Israel's population will cross the 10 million level within a decade. *(http://www.haaretz.com/israel-news/.premium-1.675203)*

Due to the alarming increase of global anti-Semitism coupled with anti-Zionism, *'aliyah'* is expected to increase. On January 25th, 2015 the Jewish Press posted the following articles on their website: *(http://www.jewishpress.com/news/israel/aliyah-israel/)*

- PM Netanyahu Calls on French Jews to Come Home to Israel
- Prime Minister Netanyahu's Remarks: *Prior to Cabinet Meeting: Prior to Sunday's cabinet meeting, Bibi talked about the dangers of Iran, ISIS and anti-Semitism and the importance of Aliyah."*
- Jewish Agency Planning for Massive Aliyah of 120,000 French Jews
- Exodus from France Leads Aliyah to 10-Year High

Following the Paris attacks on Friday, November 13, 2015, 80% of Jewish people are now considering emigration from France to Israel. The government of Israel is preparing for a massive wave of aliyah from France and Europe as well.

The Jewish people are returning to Israel, their ancient Biblical homeland. In part, anti-Semitism and persecution are driving them back home. Gentiles are responding to the beckoning call of the God of Israel to assist in *'aliyah.'* This is another one of the tangible ways to bless Israel.

LET US GO WITH YOU

Zechariah 8:23 *"Thus says the Lord of hosts: 'In those days ten men from every language of the nations shall grasp the sleeve of a Jewish man, saying,* **'Let us go with you, for we have heard that God is with you.'"**

The hour is late! The time is far spent! The culmination of all things is close at hand. The rapid rise of global terrorism, anti-Semitism and many terrorist organizations such as ISIS, Hezbollah, Hamas, Al Qaeda, Muslim Brotherhood, Boko Haram, Palestinian Liberation Front and unbelievably numerous other terrorist organizations is alarming! Many Islamic nations and terrorist organizations are openly calling for the destruction of Israel and actively engaged in advancing a global caliphate.

As in the days leading up to the Holocaust, anti-Semitism is rising today. Many have stated that during the Holocaust, if the Jewish people had their own homeland, there might not have been a holocaust. Today the Jewish people are back in their homeland. They must keep their homeland. Having a land of their own is a contributing factor to their protection and self-preservation as a people.

The nations are being weighed in the balance. Which way will the pendulum swing for you and/or your nation?

Matthew 25:40 *"Assuredly, I say to you,* **inasmuch as you did it to one of the least of these My brethren, you did it to Me."**

Individuals and nations must and will choose whether by choice or by default. Now is the time to bless Israel. Now is the time to align with the Word of God and come alongside the people of the land of Israel to bless, to serve, to love, to comfort and support the people and the nation God loves.

God's Word is clear. Will you accept Heaven's invitation to participate in ~ *God's Noble Theme?*

CHAPTER TWO 2

GOD'S COVENANT LAND

Genesis 12:1-3,7 *"The LORD had said to Abram, "Go from your country, your people and your father's household **to the land** I will show you. "I will make you into a great nation, and I will bless you; I will make your name great, and you will be a blessing. I will bless those who bless you, and whoever curses you I will curse; and **all peoples on earth will be blessed through you.** The LORD appeared to Abram and said, "To your offspring I will give this land…"* (NIV)

Genesis 13:14-17 *"And the LORD said to Abram, after Lot had separated from him: "Lift your eyes now and look from the place where you are - northward, southward, eastward, and westward; **for all the land which you see I give to you and your descendants forever.** And I will make your descendants as the dust of the earth; so that if a man could number the dust of the earth, then your descendants also could be numbered. Arise, walk in the land through its length and its width, for I give it to you."*

The land of Israel is the only place on earth that God identifies as His Land. Though the entire *"earth is the Lord's and the fullness thereof,"* it is the land of Israel that God calls His land. It's a land He loves and cares for. It is a land He jealously watches over.

Deuteronomy 11:11,12 *"...but the land which you cross over to possess is a land of hills and valleys, which drinks water from the rain of heaven,* **a land for which the LORD your God cares;** *the eyes of the LORD your God are always on it, from the beginning of the year to the very end of the year."*

THE COVENANT LAND BELONGS TO GOD

Psalm 24:1 *"The earth is the LORD's, and all its fullness, the world and those who dwell therein."*

The context of verse 23 in the Hebrew Scriptures of Leviticus 25:8-24 is in reference to the year of Jubilee. Though the land belongs to the Lord, He gave it to Abraham and his seed. The Jewish people could buy and sell property but always with the Jubilee year in mind at which time, the 50th year, all properties were returned to the original allotment of the twelve tribes. The Israelites knew that they were but stewards or tenants of God's covenant land and that God was the true Owner.

Leviticus 25:23 *"The land shall not be sold permanently, for the land is Mine; for you are strangers and sojourners with Me."*

THE JEWISH PEOPLE HAVE A BIBLICAL RIGHT TO THE LAND

God gave His land to Abraham and his descendants forever! A few years ago, while leading a mission in Israel, I brought my group to Ariel, a Jewish Settlement, in what the world calls the *'West Bank.'* The Jewish mayor of that city addressed our group holding a Bible in His hand. He proudly stated, *"Israel is the only nation that has its title deed in the Bible."*

The Word of God stands as truth! His Word is forever settled in Heaven. If God makes a statement, a statute, a decree or an ordinance, I for one believe it. It only needs to be stated once. God mentions hundreds of times throughout scripture that the rightful owners of His covenant land are the seed of Abraham. As the familiar adage goes, *"God said it. I believe it. That settles it."*

O nations of the world, hear the Word of the Lord. Israel has a Biblical right to the land!

God had a Master plan, a *Noble Theme*. His eyes went to and fro across the face of the earth seeking out someone worthy to carry out His plan. He found and chose Abram, from the Ur of the Chaldeans, and from the land of Haran to go to the land that God Himself would show him. Giving the land to Abram was God's idea. A sacred trust was being bestowed upon Abram and his descendants as an eternal inheritance. Not only to be custodians and keepers of God's land but to walk in covenant with God and steward His plans and purposes, to be a light to all nations. (Isaiah 49:6)

God gave the land of Israel to Abraham (Abram's name was changed to Abraham ~ Gen. 17:5) and his seed Isaac and Jacob, as an everlasting heritage. God's covenant was unconditional. There are over 170 scriptures in the Bible that state to whom the land belongs. God confirmed His covenant with *'an oath'* 55 times in the Bible. It is recorded 12 times in scripture that the covenant was a *'lasting ordinance'* ~ forever! Suffice it to say, to list all of the verses is not necessary.

> **Psalm 105:8-11** *"He remembers* **His covenant** *forever, The word which He commanded, for a thousand generations, The* **covenant which He made with Abraham**, *and* **His oath to Isaac**, *and confirmed it to* **Jacob for a statute**, *to Israel as an everlasting covenant, saying,* **"To you I will give the land of Canaan as the allotment of your inheritance."**

> **Genesis 12:1-3** *"The LORD had said to Abram, "Go from your country, your people and your father's household* **to the land** *I will show you. "I will make you into a great nation, and I will bless you; I will make your name great, and you will be a blessing. I will bless those who bless you, and whoever curses you I will curse; and* **all peoples on earth will be blessed through you.***"* (NIV)

God's intention and purpose of heart was to bring a people unto Himself and through this people bring all mankind from every nation of the earth unto Himself. God made promises to Abram that were irrevocable. God made eight promises to Abram in His covenant:

1) **I will show you a land:** God called Abram out of the Ur of the Chaldees and called him to leave his family. God was faithful to lead Abram to the land of Canaan.

2) **I will make you a great nation:** God was not only promising to make a great nation, but was promising seed to Abram that would be as numerous as the stars.

3) **I will bless you:** God promised material and spiritual blessing beyond what Abram could have imagined at that time.

4) **I will make your name great:** God promised to make Abram's name great and honored and revered on earth.

5) **You shall be a blessing:** God promised to make Abram a blessing in the earth, a reflection of the nature and character and glory of God.

6) **I will bless those who bless you:** God promised to pour out His blessings on all those who would bless Israel.

7) **I will curse him who curses you:** The judgment of a jealous God would fall upon individuals or nations that would curse Israel.

8) **I will bless all the families of the earth through you:** It was God's intent that *'all'* families on earth would be blessed. His blessings would flow through His chosen people.

Israel has been a blessing in all the earth! On the 'Israel21c' website, the following is stated:

"Israel has been and continues to be an incredible blessing in the earth. In little less than half a century, Israel has developed a vibrant democracy, a sophisticated industrial infrastructure and has grown a dynamic nation with global impact. Israel has also acquired a reputation for cutting-edge innovation across a wide range of disciplines – from science and technology, to agriculture, medicine, education and the arts. The beneficial results are felt around the world enhancing the lives of millions of people in virtually every corner of the world! More than six decades after Israel became an independent State in May 1948, the Israelis have turned their country into a growing source of technology and innovation. With the most start-up companies per capita worldwide, and the third highest number of patents per head, Israel has become one of the leading players in the world of high-tech innovation, attracting international giants to its shores. From health breakthroughs to technology, agriculture, the environment and the arts, the country's innovations are transforming and enriching lives everywhere. Israel today is playing a significant role in some of the most important challenges facing our planet."

(http://www.israel21c.org/technology/innovation/made-in-israel-the-top-64-innovations-developed-in-israel/)

Another amazing way that Israel has been a blessing on the earth is its numerous responses to calamities and crisis in the world such as in the tragic 7.8 earthquake in Nepal on April 25th, 2015. Tragically, 9,000 people perished and more than 23,000 were injured. Israel, as always, was one of the first responders with medical and humanitarian aid. Within 48 hours, after assessing the situation, Israel...

- deployed a delegation of 260 trained IDF humanitarian aid specialists
- sent 15 search and rescue specialists
- delivered 95 tons of equipment and humanitarian aid
- within hours, set up a make shift hospital and treated 1,600+ patients
- performed 85+ medical surgeries
- delivered 8 babies

Israel's President Rivlin said:

> "This delegation of 'messenger angels' represents the universal values, in the spirit of our people and our country."

Prime Minister Netanyahu said:

> "This is the true face of Israel - a country that offers aid over any distance at such moments."

(http://mfa.gov.il/MFA/PressRoom/2015/Pages/Israel-responds-to-earthquake-in-Nepal-25-Apr-2015.aspx)

Dozens of countries send rescue teams to disaster areas around the world but none compare to Israel's professional, devoted and experienced doctors and specialists. Reporting from Kathmandu, a Nepalese Army officer said to the arriving Israeli delegation, *"We knew you'd come. You are the best army in the world."*
(http://www.ynetnews.com/articles/0,7340,L-4652206,00.html)

QUOTABLE QUOTES

Winston S. Churchill (British Prime Minister): Some people like the Jews, and some do not. But no thoughtful man can deny the fact that they are, beyond any question, the most formidable and most remarkable race which has appeared in the world.

John Adams (U.S. President): I will insist the Hebrews have contributed more to civilize men than any other nation. If I was an atheist and believed in blind eternal fate, I should still believe that fate had ordained the Jews to be the most essential instrument for civilizing the nations ... They are the most glorious nation that ever inhabited this earth. The Romans and their empire were but a bubble in comparison to the Jews. They have given religion to three-quarters of the globe and have influenced the affairs of mankind more and more happily than any other nation, ancient or modern.

Paul Johnson (Historian, author): It is almost beyond our capacity to imagine how the world would have fared if they (the Jews) had never emerged. Certainly the world without the Jews would have been a radically different place. Humanity might have stumbled upon all the Jewish insights but we cannot be sure. To them we owe the equality before the law, sanctity of life, dignity of the human person, social responsibility, and peace as an idea and may other items which constitute the basic furniture of the human mind. Without it the world might have been a much emptier place.

John F. Kennedy (U.S. President): Israel was not created in order to disappear ~ Israel will endure and flourish. It is the child of hope and the home of the brave. It can neither be broken by adversity nor demoralized by success. It carries the shield of democracy and it honors the sword of freedom.

Sir Thomas Newton (Bishop of Bristol): The preservation of the Jews is really one of the most single and illustrious acts of divine providence. What but a supernatural power could have preserved them in such a manner as no other nation has been preserved. And no less remarkable is the destruction of their enemies. Let it serve as a warning to all those at any time or occasion are raising a clamour or persecution against them.

Woodrow Wilson (U.S. President): The laws of Moses contributed suggestions and impulses to the men and institutions which were to prepare the modern world and if we could but have the eyes to see we should readily discover how much besides religion we owe to the Jews.

David Lloyd George (British Prime Minister): Of all the extreme fanaticism which plays havoc in man's nature, there is not one as irrational as anti-Semitism.

Leo Tolstoy (Russian author): What is the Jew?... What kind of unique creature is this whom all the rulers of all the nations of the world have disgraced and crushed and expelled and destroyed; persecuted, burned and drowned, and who, despite their anger and their fury, continues to live and to flourish. What is this Jew whom they have never succeeded in enticing with all the enticements in the world, whose oppressors and persecutors only suggested that he deny (and disown) his religion and cast aside the faithfulness of his ancestors?! The Jew - is the symbol of eternity. ... He is the one who for so long had guarded the prophetic message and transmitted it to all mankind. A people such as this can never disappear.

Mark Twain (American author): If statistics are right, the Jews constitute but one percent of the human race. It suggests a nebulous dim puff of stardust lost in the blaze of the Milky Way. Properly, the Jew ought hardly to be heard of, but he is heard of, has always been heard of. He is as prominent on the planet as any other people, and his commercial importance is extravagantly out of proportion to the smallness of his bulk. His contributions to the world's list of great names in literature, science, art, music, finance, medicine, and abstruse learning are also away out of proportion to the weakness of his numbers. He has made a marvelous fight in this world, in all the ages; and had done it with his hands tied behind him. He could be vain of himself, and be excused for it. The Egyptian, the Babylonian, and the Persian rose, filled the planet with sound and splendor, then faded to dream-stuff and passed away; the Greek and the Roman followed; and made a vast noise, and they are gone; other people have sprung up and held their torch high for a time, but it burned out, and they sit in twilight now, or have vanished. The Jew saw them all, beat them all, and is now what he always was, exhibiting no decadence, no infirmities of age, no weakening of his parts, no slowing of his energies, no dulling of his alert and aggressive mind. All things are mortal but the Jew; all other forces pass, but he remains.

Quote: There is a famous story in which the Kaiser asks Bismarck, *"Can you prove the existence of God?" Bismarck replies, "The Jews, your majesty, the Jews."*

Theodor Herzl (Father of modern Zionism): The Jews who will it shall achieve their State. We shall live at last as free men on our own soil, and in our own homes peacefully die. The world will be liberated by our freedom, enriched by our wealth, magnified by our greatness. And whatever we attempt there for our own benefit will redound mightily and beneficially to the good of all mankind.

BACK TO THE COVENANT

Abram was not looking for a land grab. It was God's idea to bring him out of the land of Ur of the Chaldeans to the land that He chose. This is the first mention of God's intention to build a nation, make their name great and do so in a very specific and divinely chosen land.

> **Genesis 12:7** *"Then the LORD appeared to Abram and said, 'To your descendants **I will give this land.**' And there he built an altar to the LORD, who had appeared to him."*

God promises Abram that he would have children and they would inherit the land. Abram was 75 years old at the time. Abram responded by building an altar and worshipping God.

> **Genesis 12:4** *"So Abram departed as the LORD had spoken to him, and Lot went with him. And Abram was seventy-five years old when he departed from Haran."*

> **Genesis 13:14,15** *"And the LORD said to Abram, after Lot had separated from him: "Lift your eyes now and look from the place where you are-northward, southward, eastward, and westward; for **all** the land which you see **I give to you and your descendants forever.**"*

After a few years in the land of Canaan, Abram and his nephew Lot separated, God showed Abram for the first time, the extent of the land that he and his descendants had inherited. Abram stood and beheld the promised land of God. I can only imagine the thought swirling in God's heart as he stood by and watched Abram beholding His dream as it moved one step closer to it becoming a reality. I am sure Heaven rejoiced and the angels bore witness to all that God had purposed. God's *Noble Theme* was moving forward.

> **Genesis 13:17** *"Arise, walk in the land through its length and its width, **for I give it to you.**"*

The land was being possessed one step at a time. The dream was materializing as Abram walked the length and the width in the land. God smiles!

God put Abram into a deep sleep and cut a covenant with him.

Genesis 15:1-7 *"After these things the word of the LORD came to Abram in a vision, saying, 'Do not be afraid, Abram. I am your shield, your exceedingly great reward.' But Abram said, 'Lord GOD, what will You give me, seeing I go childless, and the heir of my house is Eliezer of Damascus?' Then Abram said, 'Look, You have given me no offspring; indeed one born in my house is my heir!' And behold, the word of the LORD came to him, saying, 'This one shall not be your heir, but one who will come from your own body shall be your heir.' Then He brought him outside and said, 'Look now toward heaven, and count the stars if you are able to number them.' And He said to him, 'So shall your descendants be.' And he believed in the LORD, and He accounted it to him for righteousness. Then He said to him, 'I am the LORD, who brought you out of Ur of the Chaldeans, to **give you this land** to inherit it.'"*

Genesis 15:17-21 *"And he said, "Lord GOD, how shall I know that I will inherit it?" So He said to him, "Bring Me a three-year-old heifer, a three-year-old female goat, a three-year-old ram, a turtledove, and a young pigeon. Then he brought all these to Him and cut them in two, down the middle, and placed each piece opposite the other; but he did not cut the birds in two. And it came to pass, when the sun went down and it was dark, that behold, there appeared a smoking oven and a burning torch that passed between those pieces. On the same day the LORD made a covenant with Abram, saying: **'To your descendants I have given this land**, from the river of Egypt to the great river, the River Euphrates - the Kenites, the Kenezzites, the Kadmonites, the Hittites, the Perizzites, the Rephaim, the Amorites, the Canaanites, the Girgashites, and the Jebusites.'"*

Genesis 28:4 *"And give you (Jacob) the blessing of Abraham, to you and your descendants with you, that you may **inherit the land** in which you are a stranger, which God gave to Abraham."*

1 Chronicles 16:13-18 *"O seed of Israel His servant, you children of Jacob, His chosen ones! He is the LORD our God; His judgments are in all the earth. Remember His covenant forever, the word which He commanded, for a thousand generations, the covenant which He made with Abraham, and His oath to Isaac, and confirmed it to Jacob for a statute, to Israel for an **everlasting covenant**, Saying, "**To you I will give the land of Canaan as the allotment of your inheritance.**"*

Exodus 6:4 *"I have also established **My covenant** with them, **to give them the land of Canaan**, the land of their pilgrimage, in which they were strangers."*

Isaiah 60:21 *"Also your people shall all be righteous; **They shall inherit the land forever**, the branch of **My planting**, the work of **My hands**, that I may be glorified."*

God's covenant land was given to the descendants of Abraham.

Genesis 12:7 *"Then the LORD appeared to Abram and said, "To your descendants I will give this land."*

God ratified His covenant once more, after Ishmael was born to Abram and Hagar. God was very specific as to whom He named as heir to His covenant land. The land was to be given to the descendants of Isaac, not Ishmael. It appears as though Abraham was thinking that Ishmael might be the heir. Indeed, God promised a great blessing for Ishmael but clearly indicated Isaac to be the heir to the everlasting covenant.

Genesis 17:18-21 *"And Abraham said to God, "If only Ishmael might live under your blessing! Then God said, "Yes, but your wife Sarah will bear you a son, and you will call him Isaac. I will establish my covenant with him as an everlasting covenant for his descendants after him. And as for Ishmael, I have heard you: I will surely bless him; I will make him fruitful and will greatly increase his numbers. He will be the father of twelve rulers, and I will make him into a great nation. But my covenant I will establish with Isaac, whom Sarah will bear to you by this time next year."* (NIV)

In like manner, God ordained that the chosen sons of the family line, down through the generations would inherit the covenant blessings as with the two sons of Isaac. God clearly intended that Jacob and His descendants would receive the covenant blessing and land, not Esau!

Israel is known both as the Holy Land and the Promised Land. The difference between the two is that the Holy Land is holy to many but the Promised Land is promised only to the Jewish people!

> *"Prime Minister Benjamin Netanyahu and his wife Sara hosted a special meeting of the Tanakh (Bible) Study Circle in honor of the Jewish New Year, Rosh Hashana (5776) in the Prime Minister's Residence.*
>
> *Netanyahu spoke of the crucial significance the Bible has to the Jewish presence in the Holy Land. "Whoever participates in this Circle on a regular basis knows that I once said that **the Tanakh is the rock of our existence… there is no other significance to our being here without our link to our Land and this Book.**"*
>
> *(http://unitedwithisrael.org/netanyahu-bible-is-rock-of-our-existence/?utm_source=MadMimi) Sept. 6, 2015*

THE COVENANT LAND SPECIFIC BOUNDARIES

Genesis 15:18-21 *"On the same day the LORD made a covenant with Abram, saying: **'To your descendants I have given this land**, from the river of Egypt to the great river, the River Euphrates- the Kenites, the Kenezzites, the Kadmonites, the Hittites, the Perizzites, the Rephaim, the Amorites, the Canaanites, the Girgashites, and the Jebusites.'"*

The land mass was huge, particularly in comparison to the land of Israel today. The Lord unmistakably and quite intentionally defined the borders from the River of Egypt to the Euphrates River and the Great Sea (the Mediterranean Sea) all the way to the land of the Hittites in the north.

God's Covenant Land

The Divine Architect and Creator defined Israel's borders! For whatever reasons God had in His plans and purposes, He did not intend for the Promised Land to extend further or be diminished by one square inch. One day all the land will be reclaimed.

Today the land mass in Israel is about one third of the original land given to Abram and his descendants. The boundaries of the land of Israel are on the bargaining table and the nations of the world are attempting to move its boundaries and carve up God's covenant land.

Of interest, is a proclamation that was made at the Third International Christian Zionist Congress held in Jerusalem, February 25-29, 1996. The Congress was attended by approximately 1500 delegates and participants representing over 40 countries. One of the articles in the Proclamation states:

> *"According to G-D's distribution of nations, the land of Yisrael has been given to the Jewish people by G-D as an everlasting possession by an eternal covenant. The Jewish people have the absolute right to possess and dwell in the land, including Judea, Samaria, Gaza and the Golan."*
>
> *(http://www.internationalwallofprayer.org/A-013-1-Proclamation-of-Third-Intl-Congress.html)*

This does not even include all of the Transjordan land that God promised Abram.

Fifty-five times in scripture, the Bible states that God swore an 'oath' to give Abram and his descendants the land. An oath is a binding sworn affirmation, a pledge, a word of honor to a solemn promise between two parties. That is about as binding as you can get!

> **Genesis 50:24** *"And Joseph said to his brethren, "I am dying; but God will surely visit you, and bring you out of this land to the land of which **He swore** to Abraham, to Isaac, and to Jacob."*

> **Exodus 6:8** *"I will bring you into the land which **I swore** to give to Abraham, Isaac, and Jacob; and I will give it to you as a heritage: I am the LORD."*

> **Exodus 13:11** *"And it shall be, when the LORD brings you into the land of the Canaanites, as **He swore** to you and your fathers, and gives it to you,"*
>
> **Deuteronomy 1:8** *"See, I have set the land before you; go in and possess the land which the **LORD swore** to your fathers—to Abraham, Isaac, and Jacob—to give to them and their descendants after them."*

God clearly states in the Book of Proverbs that the ancient landmarks, boundaries, borders and property lines are not to be removed ~ how much more the boundaries that God Himself has divinely and sovereignly set over the nation of Israel, over the land divinely allotted to Israel as their covenant land of eternal inheritance.

> **Proverbs 22:28** *"Do not remove the ancient landmark which your fathers have set."*

ISRAEL HAS AN HISTORICAL RIGHT TO THE LAND

Israel is a land and a people! The roots of the Jewish people in the Land of Israel are deep and span some 3500 years. In the land of Israel, its cultural, national and religious identity was formed. Israel indeed has an historical right to the land.

A Jewish presence has been unbroken and maintained throughout the centuries even after the Jewish people were exiled to Babylon. The Babylonian captivity took place around 586 BCE and lasted 70 years. After the return, under the leadership of Ezra and Nehemiah, the Jewish people repaired the Temple, rebuilt the walls of their beloved Jerusalem, raised up its ruins and repopulated that land. The Second Temple era spanned 420 years, ending with the Romans' destruction of the Temple in 70 CE.

Completely and entirely supported by numerous historical evidences, the Jewish people have lived in the land of Israel continuously from the time of its original conquest by Joshua more than 3200 years ago until this present day.

THE HISTORY OF JERUSALEM

- Chalcolithic Period (4500-3200 BCE) - (3500 BCE) - First Settlement of Jerusalem
- Early Bronze Age (3200-2220 BCE) - (2500 BCE) - First Houses Built in Area
- Middle Bronze Age (2220-1550 BCE) - (1800 BCE) - Construction of First City Wall
- Late Bronze Age (1400 BCE) - First Mention of Jerusalem in Cuneiform Amarna Letters
- Iron Age I (1200-1000 BCE) - (1200 BCE) - Jerusalem is conquered by Canaanites (Jebusites)
- Iron Age II (1000-529 BCE)
- (1000 BCE) - King David Conquers Jerusalem; Declares City Capital of Jewish Kingdom
- (960 BCE) - David's Son, King Solomon, Builds First Jewish Temple
- (721 BCE) - Assyrians Conquer Samaria; Refugees Flee to Jerusalem and City Expands onto Western Hill
- (701 BCE) - Assyrian Ruler Sennacherib Lays Siege to Jerusalem
- (586 BCE) - Babylonian Forces Destroy Jerusalem-Demolish First Temple Persian Period (539-322 BCE)
- (539 BCE) - Persian Ruler Cyrus the Great Conquers Babylonian Empire, Including Jerusalem
- (516 BCE) - Cyrus Permits Jews in Babylonian Exile to Return to Jerusalem; Second Temple Built
- (445-425) - BCE Nehemiah the Prophet Rebuilds the Walls of Jerusalem;
- (332 BCE) - Greek Leader Alexander the Great Conquers Judea and Jerusalem
- (332-141 BCE) - Ptolemaic and Seleucid Rule in Jerusalem Hasmonean Period (141-37 BCE)
- (141 BCE) - Hasmonean Dynasty Begins; Jerusalem Again Expands Limits to Western Hill
- (63 BCE) - Roman General Pompey captures Jerusalem Herodian Period (37 BCE - 70 CE)
- (37 BCE) - King Herod Restructures Second Temple, Adds Retaining Walls
- (30 BCE) - Jesus Crucified by Romans in Jerusalem Roman Period (70 - 324 CE)
- (70 CE) - Roman Forces Destroy Jerusalem and Demolish Second Temple
- (135 CE) - Jerusalem Rebuilt as a Roman City Byzantine Period (324-638 CE)
- (335 CE) - Church of the Holy Sepulchre Built
- (614 CE) - Persians Capture Jerusalem
- (629 CE) - Byzantine Christians Recapture Jerusalem from Persians First Muslim Period (638-1099 CE)
- (638 CE) - Caliph Omar Enters Jerusalem
- (661-750 CE) - Jerusalem Ruled Under Umayyad Dynasty
- (691 CE) - Dome of the Rock Built on Site of Destroyed Jewish Temples
- (750-974 CE) - Jerusalem Ruled Under Abassid Dynasty Crusader Period (1099-1187 CE)
- (1099 CE) - First Crusaders Capture Jerusalem Ayyubid Period (1187-1259 CE)

- (1187 CE) - Saladin Captures Jerusalem from Crusaders
- (1229-1244 CE) - Crusaders Briefly Recapture Jerusalem Two Times Mamluk Period (1250-1516)
- (1250 CE) - Muslim Caliph Dismantles Walls of Jerusalem; Population Declines
- (1517 CE) - Ottoman Empire Captures Jerusalem
- (1538-1541 CE) - Suleiman the Magnificent Rebuilds the Walls of Jerusalem British Mandate (1917-1948)
- (1917 CE) - British Capture Jerusalem in World War I Divided City (1948-1967)
- (1948 CE) - State of Israel established
- (1967 CE) - Israel Captures Jerusalem's Old City and Eastern Half; Reunites City

(http://www.jewishvirtuallibrary.org/jsource/Peace/jerutime.html)

RESTORATION OF THE LAND OF ISRAEL

In the book of Ezekiel, God speaks through His prophet promising to bring the captives of Jacob back to their land.

> **Ezekiel 39:25** *"Therefore thus says the Lord GOD: 'Now I will bring back the captives of Jacob, and have mercy on the whole house of Israel; and I will be jealous on the whole house of Israel and will be jealous for my Holy Name,"*

The following chapters of the book of Ezekiel are about the restoration of the land and the allotment to the 12 tribes of Israel. The parameters are laid out for the Third Temple and the division to the Levites and Priests. Even in this vision of the return and restoration, the land is not to be sold or exchanged ~ any of it! The portion he is speaking of in verse 13 and 14 is the place of God's sanctuary, the temple Mount in Jerusalem.

> **Ezekiel 48:13,14** *"Opposite the border of the priests, the Levites shall have an area twenty-five thousand cubits in length and ten thousand in width; its entire length shall be twenty-five thousand and its width ten thousand. **And they shall not sell or exchange any of it; they may not alienate this best part of the land, for it is holy to the LORD.**"*

ISRAEL HAS AN ARCHEOLOGICAL RIGHT TO THE LAND

The archeological evidence that has been and continues to be discovered in the land of Israel today bears witness to the Jewish presence in the land for centuries and millennia. All the archeological digs and findings support the case for the Jewish people belonging in the land of Israel. With every successive dig, new evidence supports the fact that Israelis have had a presence in Israel for more than 3,000 years. The coins, the jewelry, the pottery, the clothing, the temple seals, the cities unearthed, unmistakably validate the Jewish claim to the land. This predates the claims made by other people groups in the region.

Many nations laying claim to the land of Israel became extinct. The ancient Philistines are extinct. Others claiming ownership of the covenant land do not have an unbroken presence like the Jewish people. The Israelis of today are undeniably descended from the sons of Abraham.

The Jerusalem Post has published numerous articles about the recent archeological digs and discoveries and have stored those articles in the JP archives.

The most fascinating recent archeological discoveries in Israel were undertaken in Jerusalem around the Temple Mount. The following article was taken from the Jewish Virtual Library:

(http://www.jewishvirtuallibrary.org/jsource/Archaeology/templemountgarbage.html)

> ***Temple Mount Artifacts Saved from Garbage Heap (October 2005)*** *"In April 2005, a small team of Israeli archaeologists and volunteers discovered a series of relics dating back to the periods of the First and Second Temples in Jerusalem. The most startling aspect of this rare archaeological find was that it did not occur on the Temple Mount, but in piles of rubble at a garbage dump in the Kidron Valley thrown out by Islamic Waqf authorities. Under the direction of Bar Ilan University professor Dr. Gabriel Barkay, the team's discoveries are touted as the first of its kind because excavation has never been possible on the Temple Mount site."*

"The disrespect of the Temple Mount structure itself, as well as the removal of ancient Jewish artifacts, is hardly a new trend. In 1996, Islamic clerics converted two underground buildings from the Second Temple period into mosques, although they had never been mosques in the past. In 1999, the Waqf opened another exit to the mosque, at the expense of thousands of tons of artifact-rich dirt that was carried away by large trucks and dumped into the Kidron Valley. The Waqf authorities claim that the Temple Mount was an ancient mosque dating from the time of Adam and Eve, and reject any and all claims by Jews that the site is the place of both ancient Jewish temples."

"This area of the Temple Mount, known as Solomon's Stables, has been under constant reconstruction supervised by Islamic religious authorities in an effort to erase any Jewish archaeological claims to the site. The former head of the Israeli Antiquities Authority called the removal and dumping of these artifacts «an unprecedented archaeological crime.» The Bar Ilan archaeologists transferred nearly 70 truckloads of rubble from the garbage dump to the Emek Zurim National Park, and with a full view of the Temple Mount, conducted the first excavations of its kind by sifting through individual heaps of dirt."

"The archaeologists discovered some very compelling relics from the rubble, including some pottery dating back to the Bronze Age and First Temple periods. Over 100 ancient coins were also recovered, including some from the Hasmonean dynasty. One coin from the period of the First Revolt against the Romans reads «For the Freedom of Zion,» and was coined before the destruction of the Second Temple in 70 CE. Other finds include a Hasmonean lamp (ca. 165 CE-70 CE), arrowheads, an ivory comb, and figurines."

- 6th Century Engraved Gold Artifacts Unearthed (September 2013)
- 2,700 Year Old Inscribed Pottery Shard Found (August 2013)
- 2,000 Year Old Cooking Pots Uncovered (June 2013)
- 2,000 Year Old Stone Quarry Discovered (May 2013)
- Second-Temple Period Ritual Bath Uncovered (April 2013)

- First Temple-Period Water Reservoir Discovered (September 2012)
- 2,700 year-old Clay Fragment Found (May 2012)
- Ancient Hebrew Seal Found (May 2012)
- Temple Period Ritual Purity «Voucher» Discovered (December 2011)
- Artifacts Found in Ancient Drainage Channel (August 2011)
- Rare Second Temple-Period Gold Bell Discovered (July 2011)
- Ancient City Wall of Jerusalem Uncovered (February 2010)
- 2,000 Year Old Mikveh Uncovered (September 2009)
- Building Remains from First Temple Period Exposed (March 2008)

(http://www.jewishvirtuallibrary.org/jsource/Archaeology/archjertoc.html)

ISRAEL HAS A LEGAL RIGHT TO THE LAND

The Jerusalem Post, on June 14, 2012, posted an article entitled: ***Canadian Lawyer specializing in international law says Israel has an open-and-shut case when it comes to the capital.*** Excerpts from the article are as follows:

> *"Is there a simple answer to the question of who owns or has the legal right to Jerusalem? Dr. Jacques Gauthier, a Canadian lawyer who specializes in international law, answered that question on Wednesday with a resounding, "Yes," and suggested that if a theoretical court that was 100-percent objective were to study the legally relevant facts, ignoring politics, it would find unequivocally that only Israel possesses the exclusive title to Jerusalem."*

> *"Gauthier was interviewed by The Jerusalem Post during a trip he made to Israel for a June 11-12 conference highlighting Jewish claims to Jerusalem. He has been studying international law for 30 years. Gauthier's thesis is 1200 pages, weighs 10 pounds and contains over 3200 footnotes."*

> *"Gauthier, who is Christian, said that he became interested in Jerusalem's status after traveling to the city in 1982-1983. Gauthier begins his overview of the issues with Theodore Herzl in 1896-1897 and the Balfour Declaration of 1917, but the*

core of his argument and its most original aspect is the emphasis he places on the San Remo Conference of April 24-25, 1920."

(http://www.jpost.com/National-News/Forget-politics-Who-has-legal-right-to-Jerusalem)

In addition to Dr. Gauthier's research the Levy Report was recently published and also proves unequivocally that all Jewish people have a right to live and build in the land particularly the West Bank Settlements.

THE LEVY REPORT

The **Levy Report**, is an 89-page report on West Bank settlements published on 9 July 2012, authored by a three member committee:

1) Former Israeli Supreme Court justice, Edmund Levy
2) Former Foreign Ministry legal adviser, Alan Baker
3) Former deputy president of the Tel Aviv District Court, Tchia Shapira.

The committee was appointed by Israel's Prime Minister Benjamin Netanyahu in late January 2012 to investigate the legal status of so called unauthorized West Bank Jewish settlements, but also examined whether the Israeli presence in the West Bank is to be considered an occupation or not.

"The members of the committee did a faithful job in an unbiased and impeccable manner," declared Prime Minister Netanyahu. *"These are professional people who were appointed in accordance with all the necessary authorizations."*

(http://www.haaretz.com/misc/iphone-article/pm-defends-judge-levy-s-appointment-as-head-of-committee-that-legitimized-west-bank-construction.premium-1.484186)

The report concludes that Israel's presence in the West Bank is not an occupation, and that the Israeli settlements are legal under international law. It recommends the legalization of unauthorized Jewish settlement outposts by the state and provides proposals for new guidelines for settlement construction. Prime Minister Netanyahu praised the report, saying:

"In my opinion, this report is important because it deals with the legalization and the legitimization of the settlement enterprise in Judea and Samaria on the basis of facts, a variety of facts and arguments that should be seriously considered."
(http://en.wikipedia.org/wiki/Levy_Report)

HATIKVAH ~ THE HOPE
Israel's National Anthem

As long as deep in the heart,
The soul of a Jew yearns,
And forward to the East
To Zion, an eye looks
Our hope will not be lost,
The hope of two thousand years,
To be a free nation in our land,
The land of Zion and Jerusalem.

The title of Israel's national anthem is *Hatikva* which means *'The Hope.'* *Hatikva* is a deep longing and expression of the Jewish people to return to the ancient homeland of their forefathers. As mentioned earlier in this book, there are over 700 scriptures in the Old Testament of the Bible that speak of the return and restoration of the land and the people to eretz Israel in the last days. After Jerusalem and the Temple were destroyed in 70 C.E., by Titus and his Roman army, the Jewish people remained in the Diaspora for two thousand years without a land of their own. Daily, they longed and hoped for their homeland, a free nation, the land of Zion. They prayed toward Jerusalem several times a day. The words to the Israeli national anthem are deeply moving! The anthem is a cry, a hope, a passion, a dream, a desire, an anthem of the heart!

The words were penned as a nine-stanza poem by Nafti Herz Imber and were published around 1876. The exact date is unknown. The Zionist movement adopted this poem at the 18th Zionist Congress in 1933. The first stanza and refrain were adopted as the official national anthem when the State of Israel was established in 1948.

I often wondered why Israel's National Anthem had not changed nor a new anthem found to replace it since the Jewish people have returned to their homeland and the modern State of Israel has declared its independence in 1948. The reality is, that after all this time, the land is still in dispute with nations of the world pressuring Israel to give up land for illusive peace. Israel is situated in a hostile neighborhood, many of those nations not recognizing her right to the land nor her right to exist! Tyrannical regimes tout their venomous threats and rabid pronouncements to annihilate the Jewish state and wipe Israel off the face of the map.

Acts of terrorism and random acts of violence flood her streets, cafes, synagogues, ice cream parlours and wedding halls, to name a few. The existential threats of nuclear arms programs are hounding Israel every day.

Sadly, the words of *Hatikva* remain Israel's refrain, the deep longing of heart for a free nation, a land of their own in which the Jewish people can live in peace and security and safety.

And how does Israel respond today? In Prime Minister Benjamin Netanyahu's speech at the United Nations General assembly on October 1, 2015, he addressed many of these threats and spoke out boldly and courageously as Israel appointed leader ~ For Such A Time as This! Following are but a few excerpts from his outstanding address.

> *Ladies and Gentlemen, I bring you greetings from Jerusalem. The city in which the Jewish people's hopes and prayers for peace for all of humanity have echoed throughout the ages. Thirty-one years ago, as Israel's ambassador to the United Nations, I stood at this podium for the first time.*

I spoke that day against a resolution sponsored by Iran to expel Israel from the United Nations. Then as now, the UN was obsessively hostile towards Israel, the one true democracy in the Middle East. Then as now, some sought to deny the one and only Jewish state a place among the nations. I ended that first speech by saying: Gentlemen, check your fanaticism at the door.

More than three decades later, as the prime minister of Israel, I am again privileged to speak from this podium. And for me, that privilege has always come with a moral responsibility to speak the truth.

Last week, Maj. Gen. Salehi, the commander of Iran's army, proclaimed this: "We will annihilate Israel for sure. We are glad that we are in the forefront of executing the supreme leader's order to destroy Israel." And as for the supreme leader himself, a few days after the nuclear deal was announced, he released his latest book. Here it is. It's a 400-page screed detailing his plan to destroy the State of Israel.

Last month, Khamenei once again made his genocidal intentions clear before Iran's top clerical body, the Assembly of Experts. He spoke about Israel, home to over six million Jews. He pledged, "There will be no Israel in 25 years." Seventy years after the murder of six million Jews, Iran's rulers promise to destroy my country, murder my people. And the response from this body, the response from nearly every one of the governments represented here has been absolutely nothing! Utter silence! Deafening silence!

Perhaps you can now understand why Israel is not joining you in celebrating this deal. If Iran's rulers were working to destroy your countries, perhaps you'd be less enthusiastic about the deal.

If Iran's terror proxies were firing thousands of rockets at your cities, perhaps you'd be more measured in your praise. And if this deal were unleashing a nuclear arms race in your neighborhood, perhaps you'd be more reluctant to celebrate. But don't think that Iran is only a danger to Israel. Besides

Iran's aggression in the Middle East and its terror around the world, Iran is also building intercontinental ballistic missiles whose sole purpose is to carry nuclear warheads. Now remember this: Iran already has missiles that can reach Israel. So those intercontinental ballistic missiles that Iran is building – they're not meant for us. They're meant for you. For Europe. For America. For raining down mass destruction – anytime, anywhere!

Ladies and Gentlemen, It's not easy to oppose something that is embraced by the greatest powers in the world. Believe me, it would be far easier to remain silent. But throughout our history, the Jewish people have learned the heavy price of silence.

And as the prime minister of the Jewish state, as someone who knows that history, I refuse to be silent. I'll say it again: The days when the Jewish people remained passive in the face of genocidal enemies – those days are over. Not being passive means speaking up about those dangers. We have. We are. We will. Not being passive also means defending ourselves against those dangers. We have. We are. And we will. Israel will not allow Iran to break in, to sneak in or to walk in to the nuclear weapons club.

I know that preventing Iran from developing nuclear weapons remains the official policy of the international community. But no one should question Israel's determination to defend itself against those who seek our destruction. For in every generation, there were those who rose up to destroy our people. In antiquity, we faced destruction from the ancient empires of Babylon and Rome. In the Middle Ages, we faced inquisition and expulsion. And in modern times, we faced pogroms and the Holocaust. Yet the Jewish people persevered. And now another regime has arisen, swearing to destroy Israel.

That regime would be wise to consider this: I stand here today representing Israel, a country 67 years young, but the nation-state of a people nearly 4,000 years old. Yet the empires of Babylon and Rome are not represented in this hall of nations. Neither is the Thousand Year Reich. Those seemingly invincible empires are long gone. But Israel lives. The people of Israel live. **Am Yisrael Hai!** *The re-birth of Israel is a testament to the indomitable spirit of my people. For a hundred generations, the Jewish people dreamed of returning to the Land of Israel. Even in our darkest hours, and we had so many, even in our darkest hours we never gave up hope of rebuilding our eternal capital Jerusalem. The establishment of Israel made realizing that dream possible.*

It has enabled us to live as a free people in our ancestral homeland. It's enabled us to embrace Jews who've come from the four corners of the earth to find refuge from persecution. They came from war-torn Europe, from Yemen, Iraq, Morocco, from Ethiopia and the Soviet Union, from a hundred other lands. And today, as a rising tide of anti-Semitism once again sweeps across Europe and elsewhere, many Jews come to Israel to join us in building the Jewish future. So here's my message to the rulers of Iran: Your plan to destroy Israel will fail. Israel will not permit any force on earth to threaten its future.

And here's my message to all the countries represented here: Whatever resolutions you may adopt in this building, whatever decisions you may take in your capitals, Israel will do whatever it must do to defend our state and to defend our people.

And what a great future it could be. Israel is uniquely poised to seize the promise of the 21st century. Israel is a world leader in science and technology, in cyber, software, water, agriculture, medicine, biotechnology and so many other fields that are being revolutionized by Israeli ingenuity and Israeli innovation. Israel is the innovation nation. Israeli know-how is everywhere. It's in your computers, microprocessors and flash drives. It's in your smartphones, when you send instant messages and navigate your cars. It's on your farms, when you drip irrigate your crops and keep your grains and fresh produce. It's in your universities, when you study Nobel Prize-winning discoveries in chemistry and economics. It's in your medicine cabinets, when you use drugs to treat Parkinson's disease and multiple sclerosis. It's even on your plate, when you eat the delicious cherry tomato.

That too was perfected in Israel, in case you didn't know. We are so proud in Israel of the long strides our country has made in a short time. We're so proud that our small country is making such a huge contribution to the entire world.

Yet the dreams of our people, enshrined for eternity by the great prophets of the Bible, those dreams will be fully realized only when there is peace.

Here's just one absurd example of this obsession: In four years of horrific violence in Syria, more than a quarter of a million people have lost their lives. That's more than 10 times, more than 10 times the number of Israelis and Palestinians combined who have lost their lives in a century of conflict between us. Yet last year, this assembly adopted 20 resolutions against Israel and just one resolution about the savage slaughter in Syria. Talk about injustice. Talk about disproportionality. Twenty. Count them. One against Syria. Well, frankly I am not surprised.

Enough! Thirty-one years after I stood here for the first time, I'm still asking: When will the UN finally check its anti-Israel fanaticism at the door? When will the UN finally stop slandering Israel as a threat to peace and actually start helping Israel advance peace?

A thousand years before the birth of Christianity, more than 1,500 years before the birth of Islam, King David made Jerusalem our capital, and King Solomon built the Temple on that Mount. In a region plagued by violence and by unimaginable intolerance, in which Islamic fanatics are destroying the ancient treasures of civilization, Israel stands out as a towering beacon of enlightenment and tolerance.

Far from endangering the holy sites, it is Israel that ensures their safety. Because unlike the powers who have ruled Jerusalem in the past, Israel respects the holy sites and freedom of worship of all – Jews, Muslims, Christians, everyone. And that, ladies and gentlemen, will never change. Because Israel will always stay true to its values.

These values are on display each and every day: When Israel's feisty parliament vigorously debates every issue under the sun, When Israel's chief justice sits in her chair at our fiercely independent Supreme Court, when our Christian community continues to grow and thrive from year to year, as Christian communities are decimated elsewhere in the Middle East. When a brilliant young Israeli Muslim student gives her valedictorian address at one of our finest universities, And when Israeli doctors and nurses – doctors and nurses from the Israeli military – treat thousands of wounded from the killing fields of Syria and thousands more in the wake of natural disasters from Haiti to Nepal. This is the true face of Israel. These are the values of Israel. And in the Middle East, these values are under savage assault by militant Islamists who are forcing millions of terrified people to flee to distant shores.

Ten miles from ISIS, a few hundred yards from Iran's murderous proxies, Israel stands in the breach ~ proudly and courageously, defending freedom and progress.

Israel is civilization's front line in the battle against barbarism.

So here's a novel idea for the United Nations: Instead of continuing the shameful routine of bashing Israel, stand with Israel. Stand with Israel as we check the fanaticism at our door. Stand with Israel as we prevent that fanaticism from reaching your door.

Ladies and Gentlemen, Stand with Israel because Israel is not just defending itself. More than ever, Israel is defending you!

Please take the time to read or listen to Prime Minister Benjamin Netanyahu's entire address to the United Nations General Assembly. In my opinion, his address is unsurpassed. You can find it at this link on the Jerusalem Post.

(http://www.jpost.com/Israel-News/Politics-And-Diplomacy/Full-text-of-PM-Netanyahus-address-to-the-UN-General-Assembly-419717)

A CASE FOR ISRAEL

To build a case for Israel's right to her God given covenant land, warrants the necessity to defend all the legitimate, reasonable and valid claims that the Jewish people have to their ancient and ancestral homeland. The ones mentioned above are but a few ~ a Biblical right, an historical right, an archeological right and a legal right! Many other rights and legitimate claims could be added to the list, defined and defended but verily, verily, the leading most qualifying right that Israel has to its land is the Biblical right. God gave the land to Israel as an everlasting inheritance ~ period!

> **Psalm 105:8-11** *"He remembers **His covenant** forever, The word which He commanded, for a thousand generations, **The covenant which He made with Abraham**, **And His oath to Isaac**, and confirmed it to **Jacob for a statute**, to Israel as an everlasting covenant, saying, **"To you I will give the land of Canaan as the allotment of your inheritance."***

God's will and intent are clear and final. His most excellent and noble plans are laid bare. God's covenant land has and always will be a fundamental and central part of ~ ***His Noble Theme.***

CHAPTER THREE

GOD'S FAVORITE CITY
JEALOUS FOR JERUSALEM ~ ZEALOUS FOR ZION

Zechariah 1:14 *"This is what the Lord Almighty says: I am very jealous for Jerusalem and Zion."* (NIV)

Zechariah 8:2 *"This is what the Lord Almighty says: I am very jealous for Zion; I am burning with jealousy for her."* (NIV)

Jerusalem, also mentioned as Zion throughout scripture, is like no other city on earth. It stands alone as the jewel among all other cities! The single most qualifying reason, you might ask? Jerusalem is the one city that the Lord Almighty, the God of Israel, chose for Himself. He has desired Jerusalem above all other cities!

Psalm 132:13,14 *"For the LORD has chosen Zion; He has desired it for His dwelling place: This is My resting place forever; Here I will dwell, for I have desired it."*

2 Chronicles 6:6 *"But now I have chosen Jerusalem as the place for my name to be honored..."* (NLT)

Psalm 76:1,2 *"In Judah God is known; His name is great in Israel. In Salem also is His tabernacle, And His dwelling place in Zion."* (Salem is Jerusalem – author's note.)

Psalm 87:1-3 *"His foundation is in the holy mountains. The LORD loves the gates of Zion more than all the dwellings of Jacob. Glorious things are spoken of you, O city of God! Selah!"*

Joel 3:17,21 *"Then you will know that I the Lord your God dwell in Zion, my holy hill…The Lord dwells in Zion!"* (NIV)

Psalm 78:68 *"But chose the tribe of Judah, Mount Zion which He loved."*

Jeremiah 3:17 *"At that time Jerusalem shall be called The Throne of the LORD, and all the nations shall be gathered to it, to the name of the LORD, to Jerusalem."*

Jerusalem is the spiritual capital of the earth. I once heard a Rabbi speak of Jerusalem, more specifically the Temple Mount, as God's physical address on earth ~ the place of His Throne, His dwelling place.

Jerusalem is the beating heart of the nation of Israel! Could there ever be an Israel without Jerusalem? God speaks of Jerusalem…

Isaiah 62:3 *"You will be a crown of splendor in the LORD's hand, a royal diadem in the hand of your God."* (NIV)

In the last two chapters of the Bible, in the book of Revelation, Jerusalem is displayed as the crowning jewel in the culmination of God's *Noble Theme*. Jerusalem in fulfillment to many prophecies, will become *'the'* praise in all the earth.

Isaiah 62:6, 7 *"I have posted watchmen on your walls, Jerusalem; they will never be silent day or night. You who call on the LORD, give yourselves no rest, and give Him no rest till he establishes Jerusalem and makes her the praise of the earth."* (NIV)

A divine command is decreed from the lips of God. He addresses all those who call upon the Lord to give themselves no rest and to give Him no rest until He makes Jerusalem *'the'* praise of the earth. Until that expected end and the New Jerusalem has *"come down out of Heaven as a bride,"* as described in Revelation 21:2, the watchmen are to give God no rest in their intercession for His beloved city.

Isaiah 62:1 *"For Zion's sake I will not be silent, for Jerusalem's sake I will not remain quiet,* until her vindication shines out like the dawn, her salvation like a blazing torch." (NIV)

Jerusalem is the cradle of civilization! Jerusalem is the genesis of creation. Posted at three entrances to the Western Wall (retaining wall of Solomon's Temple) are identical signs that all say,

*"Jewish tradition teaches that the Temple Mount is the focal point of creation. In the centre of the mountain lies the **foundation stone of the world**. Here Adam came into being. Here Abraham, Isaac and Jacob served God. The first and second Temples were built upon this mountain. The Ark of the Covenant was set upon the foundation stone itself. Jerusalem was chosen by God as the dwelling place of the Shechinah.* **Isaiah 28:16** *"Therefore thus says the Lord God, 'Behold,* **I lay in Zion** *a stone **for a foundation**, a tried stone, a precious corner stone, a sure foundation…"*

Though the words posted at the three entranceways of the Western Wall state, *Jewish tradition teaches*, some Bible scholars can support from scripture that the Garden of Eden was located in Jerusalem. That is totally fascinating! God's redemptive plan began, progressed throughout history and will find its culmination in Jerusalem, the place of God's throne.

Jeremiah 3:17 *"At that time* **Jerusalem shall be called The Throne of the LORD***, and all the nations shall be gathered to it, to the Name of the LORD, to Jerusalem."*

Isaiah 2:1-3 *"The word that Isaiah the son of Amoz saw* **concerning Judah and Jerusalem***. Now it shall come to pass in the latter days that the mountain of the LORD's house shall be established on the top of the mountains, and shall be exalted above the hills; and* **all nations shall flow to it***. Many people shall come and say, "Come, and let us go up to the mountain of the LORD, To the house of the God of Jacob; He will teach us His ways, And we shall walk in His paths." For out of Zion shall go forth the law, and the word of the LORD from Jerusalem."*

The name Jerusalem occurs 806 times in the Bible, 660 times in the Old Testament and 146 times in the New Testament.

(http://www.biblestudytools.com/dictionaries/bakers-evangelical-dictionary/jerusalem.html)

Israel's first president, Chaim Weizmann, delivered a moving speech in Jerusalem, about Jerusalem, on December 1, 1948 just months after the modern state of Israel was established. Following is an excerpt from His speech:

> *"It is with a sense of humility and sorrow that I rise to speak here among you who have suffered so much and wrought so much during this great and tragic year. Jerusalem holds a unique place in the heart of every Jew. Jerusalem is to us the quintessence of the Palestine idea. (Israel was called Palestine at the time – author's comment) Its restoration symbolises the redemption of Israel. Rome was to the Italians the emblem of their military conquests and political organization. Athens embodies for the Greeks the noblest their genius had wrought in art and thought. To us Jerusalem has both a spiritual and a temporal significance. It is the City of God, the seat of our ancient sanctuary. But it is also the capital of David and Solomon, the City of the Great King, the metropolis of our ancient commonwealth. It is the centre of our ancient national glory. It was our lodestar in all our wanderings. It embodies all that is noblest in our hopes for the future. Jerusalem is the eternal mother of the Jewish people, precious and beloved even in its desolation."*

(http://elderofziyon.blogspot.co.il/2008/12/chaim-weizmann-on-jerusalem-december-1.html#.VLa1eJX9ljo)

JERUSALEM ~ THE CENTRE OF THE NATIONS

Ezekiel 5:5 *"This is what the Sovereign LORD says: This is Jerusalem, which **I have set in the center of the nations**, with countries all around her."*

God set Jerusalem in the centre, in the midst, of the nations in the land He chose, a place He called His own, Israel. Jerusalem was the crossroads of ancient civilizations. If you spread out a map of the nations, the Middle East is in the centre of all the eastern, western, northern and southern nations. Israel is centrally located as the navel of the nations. In the centre of Israel is the city of Jerusalem. In the centre of Jerusalem is the Temple Mount. In the centre of the Temple Mount is the foundation stone where Solomon built the Temple. In the centre of the Temple is the Holy of Holies, the place where the arc of the covenant was strategically positioned, the place of God's manifest Presence.

The Designer, Creator and Architect of this universe chose a very specific place on earth as His dwelling place and that place is Jerusalem, the Temple Mount, the place where the Ark of the Covenant resided. The site of the eternal throne of God.

The Midrash Tanuchma, Qudoshim states that the foundation stone is the place from which the world was founded.

> **2 Samuel 6:2** *"And David arose and went with all the people who were with him from Baale Judah to bring up from there the ark of God, whose name is called by the Name, the LORD of Hosts, who dwells between the cherubim."*
>
> **Isaiah 37:16** *"O LORD of hosts, God of Israel, the One who dwells between the cherubim, You are God, You alone, of all the kingdoms of the earth. You have made heaven and earth."*

It was above the Ark of the Covenant that God made His throne on earth and has appeared in His manifest glory. This was also known as His Shekinah glory which speaks of the Presence of God. One must pay very close attention to what God has to say about the place of His throne. Who can ever debate or question God's right and His choice to define the boundaries of a nation that He calls His own and the place of His habitation and where he will sit enthroned forever.

You may have a favorite city. You may have travelled the world and beheld with your own eyes the natural beauty and wonder of a thousand cities. Some cities crown majestic mountains, some cities caresse pristine lakes, many others singled out perhaps for a thousand and one magnificent and splendid reasons, captivating millions of hearts, but it was Jerusalem, *'the place'* that God chose as His favorite place.

God's describes the land that He gave to the Jewish people as their inheritance as a pleasant land, the most beautiful inheritance of any nation. Selah!

> **Jeremiah 3:19** *"I myself said, "'How gladly would I treat you like my children and give you **a pleasant land, the most beautiful inheritance of any nation.**"* (NIV)

God states in Jeremiah 33:9 that Jerusalem shall be to Him a name of joy, a praise, and an honor before all nations of the earth. He goes on the say that those who shall hear all the good that He will do to His people, shall fear and tremble for all the goodness and all the prosperity that He provides for it.

God created His chosen place on the mountain of His inheritance for His own dwelling. His hands established it!

> **Exodus 15:17** *"You will bring them in and plant them in the **mountain of Your inheritance**, in the place, O Lord, which **You have made For Your own dwelling**, The sanctuary, O Lord, which **Your hands have established.**"*

No wonder God's chosen city has been the target for destruction throughout the ages. The covenant making and covenant keeping God of Israel has chosen Zion, Jerusalem, the place of His throne where His beloved Son, His anointed Messiah, will one day rule and reign over all nations. Dark spiritual powers have stirred up many nations with a fury to come against God's Beloved City. The Jewish people, the appointed custodians of God's land, have been targeted! The nation of Israel has been targeted! Jerusalem has been targeted!

The Lord Almighty, Yahweh, has decreed and declared,

> **Psalm 2:6** *"For the Lord declares, "I have **placed my chosen king on the throne in Jerusalem, on My** holy mountain."* (NLT)

JEALOUS FOR JERUSALEM
ZEALOUS FOR ZION

God, whose name is Jealous (Exodus 34:14), is jealous for Jerusalem. He is burning with jealousy for Jerusalem.

Zechariah 1:14 *"This is what the Lord Almighty says: **I am very jealous for Jerusalem and Zion."*** (NIV)

Zechariah 8:2 *"This is what the Lord Almighty says: **I am very jealous for Zion; I am burning with jealousy for her."*** (NIV)

God's jealousy for Jerusalem ought to arrest us. One must pause, meditate and enquire of the Lord. What could this possibly mean? Wouldn't you love to hear from God Himself, what *'burning with jealousy'* means to Him?

Until Heaven responds, we can only surmise. We can only imagine. In the Hebrew language, the word for *'jealous'* is *'kinah'* (Strong's 7068) which has its root meaning as: jealousy, passion, zeal, anger. When God states that he is burning with jealousy, the Hebrew language amplifies the meaning in a far greater way than any English translation. By definition then, God's jealousy is raging, angry, great, extreme and heated. We may never know this side of Heaven all that these verses fully mean regarding the burning jealousy of God for His Beloved City. Jerusalem, at times, is used as a metaphor in the Bible. Jerusalem is sometimes personified as a people or the wife of God as in Ezekiel 16.

God calls Jerusalem precious, treasured, loved, bride and valued. He is consumed with a burning jealousy for her.

In a very simplistic illustration from an earthly perspective, a force to be reckoned with is a mother bear bereft or separated from her cubs or a husband's jealousy for his wife. If God describes his jealousy with such intensity and passion, we can reasonably conclude that Jerusalem is paramount and of indescribable worth, significance and value to Him.

It is noteworthy that there is only one place on earth, that God mentions in scripture that He chose to put His Name, His heart and His eyes forever. That place is Jerusalem, the place He chose for Himself, on His Holy Mountain, where Solomon's Temple once stood, the place that His gaze was set from the time of creation and very likely from before the foundations of the world. The following scripture was given to King Solomon by God at the dedication of the First Temple.

> **2 Chronicles 7:12-16** *"...I have heard your prayer, and have **chosen this place for Myself** as a house of sacrifice. When I shut up heaven and there is no rain, or command the locusts to devour the land, or send pestilence among My people, if My people who are called by My name will humble themselves, and pray and seek My face, and turn from their wicked ways, then I will hear from heaven, and will forgive their sin and heal their land. Now My eyes will be open and My ears attentive to prayer made in this place. For now I have chosen and sanctified this house, that **My Name may be there forever; and My eyes and My heart will be there perpetually.**"*

MY NAME WILL BE THERE FOREVER

It is fascinating to note that nestled in the rugged ravines of the topography of the city of Jerusalem are Mount Moriah and Mount Zion. They are separated by three valleys: The Kidron Valley, the Tryopoeon Valley and the Hinnom Valley. From an aerial perspective, these three valleys form together in such a way that resembles the letter 'W' in our English language. The letter *'shin'* in the Hebrew language looks like a 'W' (ש). *'Shin'* in the Hebrew language represents the Name of God. Thus, carved in the landscape surrounding Jerusalem is what looks like a *'shin,'* the Name of God!

The letter *'shin'* is often inscribed on mezuzahs, which are fixed on the doorposts of Jewish homes, representing the Name of God. *'Shin'* stands for Shaddai ~ the All Sufficient One. I am sure there are many layers of interpretation and understanding as to how God has placed His eyes, heart and Name over His city. This perhaps is one very fascinating consideration of God's Name placed over His City. He has inscribed on His Holy Mountain, His imprint and His signature of ownership, His penmanship etched in stone! When God called Abram out of the land of the Ur of the Chaldeans, His gaze was fixed on Jerusalem.

Many years down the road, when God led the Israelite's out of Egypt and through the wilderness for 40 years, again his eyes and heart were set on Jerusalem.

In the Book of Deuteronomy, before the Israelites entered the Promised Land, from chapters 12-18 alone, God mentions at least 19 times the phrase: *"the place which the Lord your God chooses."* He also states at least 14 times the phrase: *"the land your God is giving you to possess for an inheritance."*

Deuteronomy 12:5 "But you shall seek *the place where the LORD your God chooses*, out of all your tribes, *to put His name for His dwelling place; and there you shall go."*

Deuteronomy 15:4 "...for the LORD will greatly bless you in *the land which the LORD your God is giving you to possess as an inheritance..."*

At a backward glance in time, Jerusalem sat alone on the barren and desolate mountain range of Moriah until, one by one, by Divine orchestration, very significant events began to unfold. Led by the Spirit of God, the patriarchs made their way *'per chance'* to a lonely mountain and wrote history. Each prophetic moment became a milestone, a stake in the ground, securing *'the place'* of destiny in the unfolding of **His-Story**! God looked down, knowing the beginning from the end, and saw the extent of all that would transpire with His chosen people in His chosen place.

Jerusalem was *'the place'* where Abraham met the King of Salem.

Genesis 14:18,19 *"Then Melchizedek, **King of Salem**, brought out bread and wine. He was the priest of God Most High. And he blessed him and said: "Blessed be Abram of God Most High, Possessor of heaven and earth."*

Jerusalem was first known as Salem in the Bible. *'Salem'* or *'shalem'* (Strong's 8004) means peace in Hebrew.

David overtook the stronghold of the Jebusites and ultimately ruled and reigned in the City of the Great King, the City of Peace.

2 Samuel 5:7 *"Nevertheless David took the stronghold of Zion (that is, the City of David)."*

Melchizedek was a prophetic representation of Yeshua, the King of Righteousness. *'Melek'* means king. *'Zedek'* means righteousness.

Hebrews 7:1-3 *"For this Melchizedek, King of Salem, priest of the Most High God, who met Abraham returning from the slaughter of the kings and blessed him, to whom also Abraham gave a tenth part of all, first being translated "King of righteousness," and then also king of Salem, meaning "King of peace," without father, without mother, without genealogy, having neither beginning of days nor end of life, but made like the Son of God, remains a priest continually."*

Abraham and Melchizedek communed in the presence of the Lord in Salem! We can envision God looking beyond that significant moment, down the corridors of time and saw His Son, on that very same holy mountain who would one day offer his body to be broken and his blood to be shed. A greater communion awaited mankind. God also saw in Melchizedek that His Son, Yeshua would be, the King of Righteousness.

Hebrews 7:17 *"For it is testified,* **"You are a priest forever according to the order of Melchizedek."**

God spoke to Abraham, several years later,

Genesis 22:2-4 *"Then He said, "Take now your son, your only son Isaac, whom you love, and go to the land of Moriah, and offer him there as a burnt offering on one of the mountains of which I shall tell you. So Abraham rose early in the morning and saddled his donkey, and took two of his young men with him, and Isaac his son; and he split the wood for the burnt offering, and arose and went to* **the place** *of which God had told him. Then on the third day Abraham lifted his eyes and saw* **the place** *afar off."*

God providentially lead Abraham to *'the place'* where He himself would provide a lamb, a prophetic picture of Yeshua, Jesus, God's sacrificial Passover Lamb who would one day give his life in *'the place'* God chose on the mountain of Moriah.

A few years later, in God's redemptive plan, He divinely led King David to purchase a piece of real estate, the threshing floor of Araunah the Jebusite. There he built an altar of sacrifice to the Lord on Mount Moriah, on an ancient threshing floor. (2 Samuel 24:18-25) I believe God looked beyond the natural and saw a short distance into the future, another altar, where His Son would be sacrificed. Yes, on the same mountain! I wouldn't be surprised if it was in the exact same place!

Sometime later, after King David conquered the Jebusite city, he renamed the city, Jerusalem. **Yerushalayim** is the most common name used for the city in the Bible and the one still used by the Jewish people and Israelis today.

The Midrash says the word derives from *'yireh'* (Strong's 3070) which means *'to see.'* Taken from the name Abraham used for it, *'God sees'* or *'Jehovah Yireh.'*

David, very specifically and precisely being led by Yahweh, chose Mount Moriah, the threshing floor of Araunah the Jebusite, as *'the place'* to build an altar to sacrifice unto the Lord.

In 2 Samuel 24, when the angel sent by God to execute judgement upon Israel because of David's sin, the judgement stopped precisely at Jerusalem. The hand of judgement was stayed precisely at the threshing floor of Araunah the Jebusite.

> **2 Samuel 24:15-16** *"So the LORD sent a plague upon Israel from the morning till the appointed time. From Dan to Beersheba seventy thousand men of the people died. And when the **angel stretched out His hand over Jerusalem to destroy it, the LORD relented from the destruction,** and said to the angel who was destroying the people, "It is enough; now restrain your hand." And **the angel of the LORD was by the threshing floor of Araunah the Jebusite."***

David purchased the land to build an altar to offer a sacrifice to Yahweh. The site became the location of the temple that Solomon, David's son built. The very place chosen to build the Temple of Adonai, the future site of the throne of God, was none other than the threshing floor of Araunah.

The threshing floor speaks of a place of sifting and judging. The chosen and appointed place of God's throne was established upon a threshing floor where one day the *'sifting of God,'* the righteous and just judgements of God would be announced and pronounced.

> **2 Samuel 24: 21-25** *"Then Araunah said, "Why has my lord the king come to his servant?" And David said, "To buy the threshing floor from you, to build an altar to the LORD, that the plague may be withdrawn from the people." Now Araunah said to David, "Let my lord the king take and offer up whatever seems good to him. Look, here are oxen for burnt sacrifice, and threshing implements and the yokes of the oxen for wood. All these, O king, Araunah has given to the king." And Araunah said to the king, "May the LORD your God accept you." Then the king said to Araunah, "No, but I will surely buy it from you for a price; nor will I offer burnt offerings to the LORD my God with that which costs me nothing." So David bought the threshing floor and the oxen for fifty shekels of silver. And David built there an altar to the LORD, and offered burnt offerings and peace offerings. So the LORD heeded the prayers for the land, and the plague was withdrawn from Israel."*

The threshing floor is likened to a place of judgement in the book of Matthew.

> **Matthew 3:12** *"His winnowing fork is in his hand, and he will clear his threshing floor, gathering his wheat into the barn and burning up the chaff with unquenchable fire."*

The full price was paid for Araunah's threshing floor. King David said he would not offer to God that which cost Him nothing. David paid fifty shekels of silver. Fifty is a significant number. It symbolizes freedom and deliverance from bondage, slavery or a burden. Every fiftieth year, the year of jubilee, was to be declared with the sounding of a trumpet (Leviticus 25:9-12) at which time debts were cancelled and inheritances were returned to their rightful owners. Silver speaks of redemption. The redemption price was necessary to buy back and return a possession to its rightful owner. The fifty shekels of silver which David paid for the threshing floor is hugely significant and rich in prophetic implications.

Not only did David pay the full price for the threshing floor, but at that very threshing floor, God too paid a great price for sin, for the redemption of mankind. God's gift of redemption was not without great cost! At the very location, the threshing floor which King David purchased for fifty shekels of silver, the future site of the altar of sacrifice would one day stand on that place and God would pay the ultimate price but not with silver or gold. The cost was the life of His Son, Yeshua, Israel's Messiah.

> **2 Chronicles 3:1** *"Then Solomon began to build the temple of the Lord in **Jerusalem** on **Mount Moriah**, where the Lord had appeared to His father David. It was on the threshing floor of Araunah the Jebusite, 'the place' provided by David."* (NIV)

THE CITY OF GOD

Psalm 48:12,13 *"Walk about Zion, and go all around her. Count her towers; Mark well her bulwarks; Consider her palaces; That you may tell it to the generation following."*

Psalm 87:3 *"Glorious things are said of you, O City of God! Selah!"* (NIV)

This verse ends with the Hebrew word *'Selah,'* (Strong's 5542) a musical term meaning to pause, to rest or to contemplate. Let us consider for a moment some of the glorious things said of Jerusalem in the Bible. Selah!

Psalm 48:1 The City of our God!
Psalm 48:2 The City of the great King!
Psalm 48:2 The Joy of the whole earth!
Psalm 48:8 The City of the Lord of hosts!
Jeremiah 3:17 The throne of the Lord!
Isaiah 1:26 The City of righteousness!
Isaiah 1:26 The faithful City!
Isaiah 52:1, Revelation 21:2 The Holy City!
Isaiah 60:14 The City of the Lord!
Isaiah 60:14 Zion of the Holy One of Israel!
Isaiah 62:4 Hephzibah! (My delight is in her)
Lamentations 2:15 The perfection of beauty!
Ezekiel 48:35 The Lord is There!
Zechariah 8:3 The City of Truth!
Zechariah 8:3 The Mountain of the Lord of hosts!
Revelation 21:2 The New Jerusalem!

The eyes of the Lord are continually on Jerusalem.

Deuteronomy 11:12 *"It is a land the Lord your God cares for. The **eyes of the Lord your God are continually on it** from the beginning of the year to its end."* (NIV)

From eternity past God's gaze was set on Jerusalem. He zealously watched over and guarded *'the place,'* His land. He saw Jerusalem from eternity past and at the dawn of creation, He also saw the glorious beauty of the New Jerusalem coming out Heaven in the last days. God's world-wide government will be supreme and the throne of the Lamb will be paramount in the New Jerusalem.

From Eden, God saw all that would transpire throughout the centuries. God saw successive invading armies trampling His courts. In the last days he saw an ancient foe hurling his hatred with full force targeting God's prize city, who would stop at nothing to take the spoils and thwart the destiny of this city.

Prime Minister Benjamin Netanyahu recently posted the following on his Twitter account:

"We are in a battle for Jerusalem, our eternal capital. There are those who would like to uproot us from our land and from our eternal capital. They will not achieve their aim. I often hear Palestinians accuse Israel of Judaizing Jerusalem ~ that is like accusing America of Americanizing Washington, or the British of Anglicising London. You know why we are called Jews? Because we come from Judea."

Israel's UN Ambassador, Ron Prosor, speaking to the US Security Council:

"I am here to convey one simple truth. The people of Israel are not occupiers and we are not settlers. Israel is our home and Jerusalem the eternal capital of our sovereign state. Throughout history, Jerusalem has been the capital for one people and only one people ~ the Jewish people. I am holding a Bible which holds almost 4,000 years of Jewish history in the land of Israel. In it we read about our forefathers ~ Abraham, Isaac and Jacob ~ who travelled Jerusalem's rolling hills. We read about King David who laid the cornerstone for His palace over 3,000 years ago. That's King David from Bethlehem not King David from the West Bank, and certainly not King David from the occupied territories. And in the Bible we read about King Solomon who constructed the First Temple, Jerusalem as a Divine promise to the Jewish people. The connection between the Jewish people and our capital cannot be denied. Nothing you can say will change that. Jerusalem is Mount Zion and Mount Moriah and the Temple Mount. To walk in this place is to follow the footsteps of our forefathers and to feel the hopes and dreams of the Jewish people....and so today I issue this promise from the people of the Promised Land ~ under our watch, Jerusalem, the eternal capital of the Jewish people will remain a free and open city for all people and for all time."

(Dispatch from Jerusalem, Publication of Bridges for Peace, February, 2015)

God gave the land to the Jewish people as their eternal inheritance.

BORDERS AND BOUNDARIES NOT TO BE MOVED

God said that he would make Jerusalem a cup of reeling, a cup of intoxication. The nations will be provoked with frenzy, madness and drunkenness in their attempt to seize Jerusalem, to capture the city, to carve it up, divide the spoils and move its boundaries.

> **Zechariah 12:2, 3** *"I am going to make **Jerusalem a cup that sends all the surrounding peoples reeling.** Judah will be besieged as well as Jerusalem. On that day when all nations of the earth are gathered against her, I will make Jerusalem an immovable rock for all the nations. **All who try to move it will injure themselves.**"* (NIV)

God will judge the nations that come against Jerusalem. He is jealously watching over and guarding Jerusalem and will execute judgement on all nations that oppose the will and Word of the Lord.

The root of the conflict is spiritual. The *'ancient foe'* will work through any nation, any people, any ideology, any dispensation to seize the covenant land and the covenant City as his trophy, his ultimate prize! The only reason the enemy has scoped out this City is because it is deemed precious and holy unto the Lord and set apart as the City of Destiny, the City of the Great King. It is God's City, pregnant with purpose and destined for Glory, the coming Messiah!

We can hold the newspaper in one hand and the Bible in the other and see the ancient prophecies being fulfilled before our very eyes.

> **Joel 3:2** *"I will also gather all nations, And bring them down to the Valley of Jehoshaphat; And I will enter into judgment with them there On account of **My people, My heritage Israel,** Whom they have scattered among the nations; They have also divided up My land."*

The leaders of the nations who seek to divide God's land are in collusion on a collision course with the God of Abraham, Isaac and Jacob.

> **Zechariah 2:8,9** *"For this is what the Lord Almighty says, 'Whoever touches you, (Israel) touches the apple of his eye - I will surely raise my hand against them'..."* (NIV)

The Biblical homeland, the eternal inheritance of the Jewish people is not intended to be an Arab nor a Muslim state nor is the eternal undivided city of Jerusalem to be the capital of a Palestinian State! The name 'Jerusalem' does not appear, not even once, in the Quran, the Muslim holy book.

THE FINAL BATTLE

The spiritual battle is intensifying over Jerusalem. Nations are raging over who will rule on Mount Zion. Jerusalem is the prize! The mother of all wars will be fought in the Jezreel Valley, also known as the Valley of Armageddon, north of Jerusalem.

Jerusalem is the only city on earth where believers are exhorted to pray for the peace of a city.

> **Psalm 122:6-8** *"Pray for the peace of Jerusalem: 'May they prosper who love you. Peace be within your walls, Prosperity within your palaces.' For the sake of my brethren and companions,* I will now say, 'Peace be within you.' "

God's *Noble Theme* for Israel and the nations will reach it's expected end! God's shalom will reign supreme on Mount Zion and sovereignly affect every nation in the world. The final battle will usher in the great reign of peace, when the Prince of Peace, Yeshua, returns to set up His throne in Jerusalem. God's plans and purposes will be fulfilled. Until that end, *"Pray for the peace of Jerusalem!"*

> **Revelation 16:16** *"And they gathered them together to the place called in Hebrew, Armageddon."*

Who can even begin to imagine the enormity and magnitude of such a cataclysmic battle with an army two hundred million coming from the east?

Revelation 9:16 *"Now the number of the army of the horsemen was two hundred million; I heard the number of them."*

In this hour, nations and individuals are being weighed in the balance! End-time nations are taking their place rapidly. We must choose and we must choose wisely. As Christians, we ought to love the things that our Heavenly Father loves and hate the things that He hates. We ought to be jealous and zealous over the same things that God is jealous and zealous over. God is jealous for Jerusalem! God is zealous over Zion!

Let us not find ourselves on the side of those seeking to move the boundaries of Jerusalem and dividing what God calls, *'My Land.'* The raw nerve of any nation attempting to divide up God's real estate and move in and take over! There is a popular Jewish/Yiddish word *'chutzpah'* derived from the Hebrew word chutzpah, meaning insolence, audacity or cheeky. The sheer chutzpah of any nation attempting to move the boundary lines of a land that God calls His own, a land with God defined borders, is incomprehensible.

God says that He is coming to judge the nations that have scattered His people and divided His land. God never intended for there to be a 'two-state solution'. He actually told the Israelites not to make an alliance, an agreement nor a covenant with the nations that He would drive out from before them.

Exodus 23:32 *"You shall make no covenant with them, nor with their gods."*

Deuteronomy 7:2 *"Make no treaty with them."* (NIV)

Abraham, Isaac and Jacob received the Promised Land from the God of Israel. As evangelical Bible believing Christians, we must not be silent. We must stand against the global and international pressures that try to delegitimize, demonize and destroy the State of Israel and divide God's covenant land. The very people sitting at the negotiation table with Israel and the nations are the Palestinians who do not even believe the Jewish people have a right to exist, let alone have a right to their ancient Biblical homeland.

Psalm 2:1-6 *"Why do the nations rage, and the people plot a vain thing? The kings of the earth set themselves, and the rulers take counsel together, Against the LORD and against His Anointed, saying, 'Let us break their bonds in pieces and cast away their cords from us.' He who sits in the heavens shall laugh; The Lord shall hold them in derision. Then He shall speak to them in His wrath, and distress them in His deep displeasure: "Yet **I have set My King on My holy hill of Zion.**"*

Psalm 83:1-5 *"Do not keep silent, O God! Do not hold Your peace, And do not be still, O God! For behold, Your enemies make a tumult; And those who hate You have lifted up their head. They have taken crafty counsel against Your people, And consulted together against Your sheltered ones. They have said, **'Come, and let us cut them off from being a nation, That the name of Israel may be remembered no more.'** For they have consulted together with one consent; they form a confederacy against You:"*

Both of these Psalms were written about 3,000 years ago. Even preceding the dates and times when these two Psalms were written, nations were stirred with an ancient hatred against God, His covenant people and His covenant land. The root of the conflict is spiritual.

Ultimately, the imminent battle will be fought in the last days. Jerusalem is fundamentally significant in God's end-time purposes. It is interesting to note that in Psalm 83, beginning with verse 6, the nations that form an unholy alliance against Israel are all nations that presently are sharing borders with Israel.

The psalmist cried out, *"Do not keep silent, O God! Do not hold Your peace, And do not be still, O God!"* The Lord will surely uphold Zion's cause.

Isaiah 34:8 *"For it is the day of the LORD's vengeance, the year of recompense for the cause of Zion."*

Isaiah 62:1 *"For Zion's sake I will not keep silent, for Jerusalem's sake I will not remain quiet, till her vindication shines out like the dawn, her salvation like a blazing torch."* (NIV)

It is noteworthy that Psalm 2 ends with an appeal:

Psalm 2:10-12 *"Now therefore, be wise, O kings; **Be instructed, you judges of the earth. Serve the LORD with fear, and rejoice with trembling. Kiss the Son, lest He be angry,** and you perish in the way, when His wrath is kindled but a little. Blessed are all those who put their trust in Him."*

God's redemptive heart implores the kings of the earth, while there is still time, to turn to Him that they might know Him and be intimately acquainted with Him.

Psalm 83:18 *"That they may know that **You**, whose Name alone is the LORD, are the Most High over all the earth."*

PRAY FOR PEACE OF JERUSALEM

Psalm 122: 6-9 *"Pray for the peace of Jerusalem: "May they prosper who love you. Peace be within your walls Prosperity within your palaces." For the sake of my brethren and companions, I will now say, "Peace be within you." Because of the house of the LORD our God I will seek your good."*

The exhortation to pray for the peace of Jerusalem is imperative in this hour. The Hebrew word for peace, *'shalom,'* (Strong's 7965) goes far beyond the first glance of an English word. It is impossible to translate the word *'shalom'* into one single English word. It is far richer and much more comprehensive in meaning. *'Shalom'* comes from the Hebrew word *'shalem'* which means everything from completeness, wholeness, soundness, health, peace, welfare, safety, preservation, perfection and harmony. A rabbi once wrote that *'shalom'* means, '*No good thing is withheld.*' Therefore, when one prays for the peace of Jerusalem, one prays also and implies that all evil, strife, violence, injustice, agitation, discord, poverty, sickness, abuse and all other forms of wickedness and evil would be absent. To pray for the peace of Jerusalem is to seek her good and ultimately see the manifestation of God's noble purposes crowned over His Beloved City. It also implies, making inquiry about Jerusalem, to inquire about the wellbeing of the City.

ARISE SHINE

Isaiah 60:1-3 *"Arise, shine; for your light has come! And the glory of the LORD is risen upon you. For behold, the darkness shall cover the earth, and deep darkness the people; But the LORD will arise over you, and His glory will be seen upon you. The Gentiles shall come to your light, and kings to the brightness of your rising."*

The unfolding of God's glorious plans for Jerusalem will reach God's stated and expected end. His glory will be manifest over His City. Jerusalem will arise victorious and shine with His splendor, brighter than the noon-day sun. The Lord will arise over Zion and many will come to the brightness of her rising.

Psalm 102:13-16 *"You will arise and have mercy on Jerusalem and now is the time to pity her, now is the time you promised to help. For your people love every stone in her walls and cherish even the dust in her streets. Then the nations will tremble before the Lord. The kings of the earth will tremble before his glory. For the Lord will rebuild Jerusalem. He will appear in His glory."* (NLT)

ZEALOUS FOR ZION
JEALOUS FOR JERUSALEM

Glorious things are said of Jerusalem. God is zealous for Zion! God is burning with jealousy for Jerusalem! His zeal is stirred! His jealous heart is stirred!

For God's Beloved City, for His noble purposes, may your heart be ~ *Stirred with the same Noble Theme!*

CHAPTER FOUR

ISRAEL AND BIBLE PROPHECY

Jeremiah 1:12 *"The LORD said to me, 'You have seen correctly, for I am watching to see that My Word is fulfilled.'"* (NIV)

The Word of the Lord came to Jeremiah saying, *"Jeremiah, what do you see?"* Jeremiah replied, *"I see a branch from an almond tree."* Then the Lord said to Jeremiah that he saw well, for the Lord was hastening to bring His Word to pass.

The Hebrew word for almond branch is *'shakeid.'* (Strong's 8247) This was a play on words. By using the almond branch in the context of the prophecy, God was clearly stating to Jeremiah that He was watching over His Word. In like manner, just as the almond branch was budding and blossoming and about to bring forth fruit, the Word of the Lord would bud and come to fruition in its fulfillment. It would come to pass in season and at the fullness of time!

BIBLE PROPHECY FULFILLED TODAY

Bible Prophecy is fascinating. Bible prophecy is God's idea. The prophecies in the Bible that have been fulfilled lend unprecedented credibility and validation to the Bible's claim that it is the Word of God. Each time a prophecy is fulfilled it attests to the precision and accuracy of Scripture. Bible prophecy speaks of appointed times where promises, decrees and judgements are foretold. Close to one third of scripture is prophetic in nature.

According to *"The Encyclopedia of Biblical Prophecy"* by J. Barton Payne, there are 1,239 prophecies in the Old Testament and 578 prophecies in the New Testament for a total of 1,817. These prophecies are contained in 8,352 of the Bible's verses. Since there are 31,124 verses in the Bible, the 8,352 verses that contain prophecy constitute 26.8 percent of the Bible's volume.

(http://gracethrufaith.com/ask-a-bible-teacher/much-bible-prophecy/)

Many scriptures have found their fulfillment in history and many await their appointed time. Years ago I heard Don Finto, author of <u>Your People Shall Be My People</u>, make a statement to the effect that every unfulfilled prophecy is an open invitation to partner with God through intercession and prayer till the promises find their fulfilment.

Both individuals and leaders today have an incredible opportunity to partner with God and align with His purposes as outlined in scripture.

Not one prophecy or Word of the Lord will fall to the ground! Not one prophecy or Word of the Lord will return to Him void. Each would find its fulfillment in God's precise time. God's *Noble Theme*, His covenants, His declarations and proclamations have been eternally recorded and are awaiting their appointed time.

> **Isaiah 55:10,11** *"For as the rain comes down, and the snow from heaven, And do not return there, But water the earth, And make it bring forth and bud, That it may give seed to the sower And bread to the eater,* ***So shall My word be that goes forth from My mouth; It shall not return to Me void,*** *But it shall accomplish what I please, And it shall prosper in the thing for which I sent it."*

ALIYAH ~ THE RETURN OF THE JEWISH PEOPLE TO THE LAND OF ISRAEL

One of the greatest modern day miracles that we bear witness to today is the restoration of the nation of Israel. God's people are back in the land in fulfilment of hundreds of prophecies found in God's Word. After two thousand years in the Diaspora, exile, the Jewish people have made aliyah to their ancient homeland, the land of their forefathers, the covenant land of their inheritance.

> **Amos 9:14,15** *"I will bring back the captives of My people Israel; They shall build the waste cities and inhabit them; They shall plant vineyards and drink wine from them; They shall also make gardens and eat fruit from them.* ***I will plant them in their land, and no longer shall they be pulled up from the land I have given them****, says the LORD your God."*

Mark Twain visited Israel in 1867. His impressions were recorded in <u>Innocents Abroad</u>. His description was dismal and foreboding. Yes, the land was desolate and mournful after the Jewish people had been exiled for almost 2,000 years.

> *"... A desolate country whose soil is rich enough, but is given over wholly to weeds... a silent mournful expanse... a desolation... hardly a tree or shrub anywhere. Even the olive tree and the cactus, those fast friends of a worthless soil, had almost deserted the country. Of all the lands there are for dismal scenery, I think Palestine must be the prince. The hills are barren, they are dull of color and they are unpicturesque in shape. The valleys are unsightly deserts fringed with a feeble vegetation that has an expression about it of being sorrowful and despondent. Palestine sits in sackcloth and ashes. Over it broods the spell of a curse that has withered its fields and fettered its energies."*

(http://www.jewishvirtuallibrary.org/jsource/Quote/innocentstoc.html)

Mark Twain's observations only confirm what the scriptures had already foretold. There would be a desolation of the land and Mark Twain bore witness to that.

> **Ezekiel 36:34-36** *"The desolate land shall be tilled instead of lying desolate in the sight of all who pass by. So they will say, 'This land that was desolate has become like the Garden of Eden; and the wasted, desolate, and ruined cities are now fortified and inhabited.' Then the nations which are left all around you shall know that I, the LORD, have rebuilt the ruined places and planted what was desolate. I, the LORD, have spoken it, and I will do it."*

Mark failed to see the Promised Land through the lense of the Hebrew prophets who foretold the time of Israel's restoration where upon the return of the Jewish people, the land would flourish and come alive, responding to the footsteps of God's Chosen People. Even the desert would blossom as a rose.

Anyone who walks the land of Israel today can and will see Bible prophecy being fulfilled! The Hebrew prophets saw this day when God would favor Zion.

> **Psalm 102:12,13** *"But You, O LORD, shall endure forever, and the remembrance of Your name to all generations.* **You will arise and have mercy on Zion; for the time to favor her, yes, the set time, has come."**

Let us rejoice that the Word of God is coming to pass and finding it's fulfillment in God's perfect plan ~ For Such a Time as This! God's *Noble Theme* is coming to pass. The faithfulness of God is bringing to pass all that He declared through the Hebrew prophets.

READING THE SIGNS ~ DISCERNING THE TIMES

It is amazing when God punctuates a prophecy with a living tangible sign that confirms His Word. The mountain fortress of Masada is the infamous place where the last Jewish zealots held their ground, so to speak, against the invading Roman armies to defend their lives and their covenant land. Tragically, close to 1000 Jewish lives ended on that mountain about three years after Jerusalem fell in 70AD.

Two thousand years later, God trumpeted a prophetic message from that mountain top when the early Zionists and pilgrims found their way back to Masada. Those who climbed the mountain fortress made an awesome discovery. It was a profound and timely prophetic statement! Those who have eyes to see and ears to hear recognize this sign as none other than the hand of God upholding His Word in a tangible way to prove Himself true and faithful to that which He proclaimed thousands of years ago about His covenant land and people.

In the ruins of the ancient synagogue, on top of the long-deserted mountain fortress of Masada, fragments of two scrolls, parts of Deuteronomy and Ezekiel 37 were found hidden in pits dug under the floor of a small room built inside the synagogue.
(https://www.jewishvirtuallibrary.org/jsource/Archaeology/Masada1.html)

They remained hidden away and preserved for centuries, just as with the discovery of the Dead Sea Scrolls in the caves of Qumran.

The Dead Sea Scrolls were discovered in 1947 by a Bedouin boy in Israel's Judean Desert. They are on display today in the Shrine of the Book at the Israel Museum in Jerusalem, (520 B.C.E.-70 C.E.)
(http://www.jewishvirtuallibrary.org/jsource/History/deadsea.html)

Imagine for a moment, of the entire written Word of God, the Ezekiel scrolls were preserved on Mount Masada. Could it be that God providentially and prophetically concealed and then revealed a scroll on Mount Masada that would speak a clear message to the nation and the world, 2000 years after its exile?

Could it be that God reserved and preserved a witness in the scrolls? If so, that God might divinely orchestrate such a thing, in such an historic place where the last Jewish presence defended their God given inheritance, is in my eyes, totally awesome. The scroll that was found, on Masada, was none other than a portion of the scrolls of the book of Ezekiel Chapter 37.

This prophecy is about the valley of dry bones! Through the discourse that Ezekiel had with God, Ezekiel was instructed to prophesy to the dry bones and then prophesy to the breath to come from the four winds and breathe into these slain, that they may live.

> **Ezekiel 37:10-14** *"So I prophesied as He commanded me, and breath came into them, and they lived, and stood upon their feet, an exceedingly great army. Then He said to me, "Son of man, these bones are the whole house of Israel. They indeed say, 'Our bones are dry, our hope is lost, and we ourselves are cut off!' Therefore prophesy and say to them, 'Thus says the Lord GOD: "Behold, **O My people, I will open your graves and cause you to come up from your graves, and bring you into the land of Israel.** Then you shall know that I am the LORD, when I have opened your graves, O My people, and brought you up from your graves. I will put My Spirit in you, and you shall live, and I will place you in your own land. Then you shall know that I, the LORD, have spoken it and performed it," says the LORD."*

"These bones are the whole House of Israel." This is absolutely amazing! After 2000 years in the Diaspora, enduring the horrors of pogroms, crusades, wanderings, expulsions, a holocaust, inquisitions and unspeakable atrocities, God brought His people back to eretz (the land of) Israel.

While in exile, the Jewish people said, *'Our bones are dried up and our hope is gone; we are cut off."* The horrors of the Holocaust was one of the darkest times not only of the Jewish people but also in the history of mankind. In the Nazi camps, Jews were treated as slaves, degraded and deprived of food and basic needs. They became walking skeletons. Many lost their hope. They felt betrayed and isolated, cut off from their families, loved ones and homes. However, from the ashes of the Holocaust and the graves of the Nazi camps, God planted the Jewish people back in their homeland never to be uprooted again. Historical facts cannot be denied. The United Nations voted to give the Jewish people their own land, recognized them as a nation and at that time, aligned with the will of God.

Isaiah released a prophecy in his day. When the Jewish people came back to their ancient homeland, God gave them beauty for ashes, the oil of joy for mourning and the garments of praise for the spirit of heaviness. God was watching over His Word to perform it!

> **Isaiah 61:3** *"To console those who mourn in Zion, to give them beauty for ashes, the oil of joy for mourning, the garment of praise for the spirit of heaviness; that they may be called trees of righteousness, the planting of the LORD, that He may be glorified."*

The second signpost, on Mount Masada, was the recent discovery of the oldest seeds ever to have been found in the world! Date palm seeds lay dormant, seemingly dead, dried up, baked and parched in the hot Judean desert for over 2000 years, far beyond the possibility of ever coming to life ~ or at least one might think! Just like the dry bones in Ezekiel's prophecy, one might conclude that the hope of finding a trace of life was impossible. I have visited Masada on numerous occasions and the temperature is often 43°C in the shade ~ not that we ever found much shade in the desert. The seeds lay patiently awaiting their appointed time of discovery, like the Dead Sea Scrolls. Just a few years ago the seeds were discovered on Masada. Could life possibly exist in a seed after that length of time? The date palm seeds were germinated in Israel, the land of miracles, planted in Israeli soil and *'voila'* a date palm tree is now thriving and towering a little over 10 feet tall. Israel has appropriately named the date palm, Methuselah, after the oldest person to have lived, as recorded in the Bible, Genesis 5:27.

(http://news.nationalgeographic.com/2015/03/150324-ancient-methuselah-date-palm-sprout-science/)

An interesting characteristic about the date palm is that this plant, particularly in ancient Biblical times, bore medicinal benefits and properties that cured many diseases and infections even promoting longevity.

(http://en.wikipedia.org/wiki/Judean_date_palm#/media/File:JudeanDatePalmMethuselah.JPG)

Could this be a prophetic parallel? Since Israel has been planted back in the land, the nation has come alive again and has been a blessing to the world through its amazing medical discoveries, it has brought blessings of healing and better quality of life. Scientific inventions, technological advancements and innovative developments from Israel have benefitted many nations of the world. Could this be a modern day fulfillment of the blessings of the Abrahamic covenant? Absolutely!

> **Genesis 12:3** *"And in you all the families of the earth shall be blessed."*

Amen! No other people group has ever been scattered among the nations of the world and come back to their ancient homeland to live, prosper and thrive, as Israel does today. The Jewish people are back in the land to stay. God Almighty has planted them there never to be uprooted again.

> **Amos 9:15** *"**I will plant them in their land, and no longer shall they be pulled up from the land I have given them**, says the LORD your God."*

PROPHETIC SIGNPOSTS FROM THE WORD OF GOD

In Jewish tradition, the public reading of portions of the *Torah* (the first five books of the Bible, written by Moses) are read in synagogues in Israel and all over the world every Shabbat (Saturday). Regular public reading of the Torah was introduced by the scribe Ezra after the return of the Judean exiles from the Babylonian captivity (c. 537 BCE) as described in the Book of Nehemiah. According to a set procedure, the Torah reading has remained unchanged since the destruction of the Temple in Jerusalem (70 CE).

The *haftarah* readings that accompany the Torah reading are a series of selections from the books of the Hebrew Prophets of the Bible that are also publicly read in synagogues. The *haftarah* reading follows the *Torah* readings on each Sabbath, Jewish festivals and fast days. Typically, the *haftarah* reading each week is thematically linked to the *Torah* portion that precedes it.

It is of great interest to pause and look at the signposts that were sovereignly planted and rooted in the scriptures of the Bible, from the *haftarah* readings on two very significant days in Israel's modern history.

On **May, 14th, 1948** Israel announced to the world its Declaration of Independence. This day is known as Yom Ha'atzmaut (Day of Independence) and is commemorated every year not only in Israel but around the world. The very day after Israel's Declaration of Independence, on Shabbat~Saturday, May 15th, the haftarah reading was read and celebrated publically. The last two verses of the Prophet Amos are:

> **Amos 9:14,15** *"'I will bring back the captives of My people Israel; They shall build the waste cities and inhabit them; They shall plant vineyards and drink wine from them; They shall also make gardens and eat fruit from them. I will plant them in their land, and no longer shall they be pulled up from the land I have given them,' says the LORD your God."*

On **June 7th, 1967**, the Israeli army recaptured their beloved City Jerusalem from the hands of the Jordanians. This day is celebrated as *Jerusalem Day* every year. The restoration of Jerusalem as Israel's capital, approximately 2,800 years after King David made it the capital, and 2,000 years after its destruction by the Roman army, led by Titus, is one of the most remarkable events in world history.

The *haftarah* reading on the week of June 7th, 1967, was from the Book of Zechariah 2:14 - 4:7.

> **Zechariah 2:12** *"And the LORD will take possession of Judah as His inheritance in the Holy Land, and will again choose Jerusalem."*

We can only stand in awe of the sovereign confirmations read in every synagogue on two of the most significant days in Israel's modern history.

OPERATION EXODUS

December 2004 marked one of the most profoundly moving experiences of my life. I boarded the Ebenezer ship at Haifa, Israel, with leaders of the Christian ministry, *Operation Exodus*. We were enroute to the ancient Port of Odessa, Ukraine. We travelled across the Mediterranean Sea, into the Aegean Sea, through the narrow Straights of the Dardanelles, into the Sea of Marmara, through very narrow Bosphorus Straight, under the Bosphorus Bridge which connects East and West Istanbul, Turkey and into the Black Sea. Our mission? To dock at Odessa port and bring 100 Russian olim (immigrants making *aliyah*) back to their ancient homeland, Israel.

It was a three and a half day journey to Odessa from the port in Haifa. On the third day, after a stormy and cloudy day on the Black Sea, the sun broke out and a magnificent rainbow arched in the horizon over the Port city of Odessa. How timely! Personally, I was reminded not only of God's covenant promise to Noah but His promises to His covenant people Israel, to bring them back to eretz Israel.

Over 100,000 Russian olim were carried back to Israel on many sailings on the Ebenezer ship from 1991 – 2004. I was on the historic last sailing. Over 1,000,000 Russian olim have emigrated either by air or sea to Israel from the former Soviet Union. God is bringing His people back home!

> **Isaiah 49:22** *"Thus saith the Lord GOD, Behold, I will lift up mine hand to the Gentiles, and set up my standard to the people: and they shall **bring thy sons in their arms, and thy daughters shall be carried upon their shoulders.***"(KJV)

That last profound and significant sailing on the Ebenezer ship is one I shall never forget. The Jewish people, whom we had the joy and privilege of assisting in making *aliyah*, left an indelible impression in my heart forever! We literally and lovingly carried the Russian Jewish children, the sons and daughters, in our arms and on our shoulders with abounding joy, fully realizing that we were fulfilling part of God's end time plans and purposes for His chosen people.

ALIYAH SCRIPTURES

> **Ezekiel 36:8** *"But you, mountains of Israel, will produce branches and fruit for my people Israel, for they will soon come home."* (NIV)

Isaiah 66:8 *"Who has heard such a thing? Who has seen such things? Shall the earth be made to give birth in one day? Or shall a nation be born at once? For as soon as Zion was in labor, she gave birth to her children."*

Can a country be born in a day? Can a nation be brought forth in a moment? The answer to both questions is a resounding, *'Yes!'* On May 14th, 1948 the modern state of Israel was reborn. God preserved his Word in a clay jar as one simple yet profound evidence that God was and is watching over His Word to fulfill it.

Isaiah 43:5,6 *"Fear not, for I am with you;* **I will bring your descendants from the east, and gather you from the west; I will say to the north, 'Give them up!' And to the south, 'Do not keep them back!' Bring My sons from afar, and My daughters from the ends of the earth."*

Jeremiah 23:3,7,8 *"But* **I will gather the remnant of My flock** *out of all countries where I have driven them, and bring them back to their folds; and they shall be fruitful and increase. "Therefore, behold, the days are coming," says the LORD, "that they shall no longer say, 'As the LORD lives who brought up the children of Israel from the land of Egypt,' but,* **'As the LORD lives who brought up and led the descendants of the house of Israel from the north country and from all the countries where I had driven them.' And they shall dwell in their own land."*

Jeremiah 32:37-41 *"Behold, I will gather them out of all countries where I have driven them in My anger, in My fury, and in great wrath; I will bring them back to this place, and I will cause them to dwell safely. They shall be My people, and I will be their God; then I will give them one heart and one way, that they may fear Me forever, for the good of them and their children after them. And I will make an everlasting covenant with them that* **I will not turn away from doing** *them good; but I will put My fear in their hearts so that they will not depart from Me. Yes,* **I will rejoice over them to do them good, and I will assuredly plant them in this land, with all My heart and with all My soul."*

God decreed that He would not stop doing good to Israel. This is the only scripture in the Bible where God says that He will do something with *'all His heart and soul.'* Bringing the Jewish people back to the land of Israel and planting them there forever is huge in God's heart. It is part of His *Noble Theme!* It is part of the blueprint and destiny of the nation. It is all about God's end time Kingdom plans and purposes for Israel and the nations of the world. The restoration of the land of Israel that we witness today is a miracle of Biblical proportions.

When Jesus was asked, *"What is the greatest commandment?"* He replied:

> **Matthew 22:37,38** *"Jesus said to him, 'You shall love the LORD your God with all your heart, with all your soul, and with all your mind.' This is the first and great commandment.'"*

> **Deuteronomy 6:4,5** *"Hear, O Israel: The LORD our God, the LORD is one! You shall* **love the LORD your** *God with all your heart, with all your soul, and with all your strength."*

These are remarkable parallel scriptures. It is with the very same zeal, the same level of commitment, passion and love that the Jewish people and Christians are asked to love God. What He asks of us, He is committed, with the very same zeal to do on behalf of His chosen people, to plant them in their land.

> **Isaiah 5:26** *"He will lift up a banner to the nations from afar, and* **will whistle to them from the end of the earth***; surely they shall come with speed, swiftly."*

There is a last day, end-time call in the Spirit, trumpeted from the heart of God. He is whistling for His people and will bring them back to the land of Israel. Some Bible translations say that God will 'signal' or *'hiss.'*

> **Zechariah 10:6,8,9** *"I will strengthen Judah and save the tribes of Joseph. I will restore them because I have compassion on them. They will be as though I had not rejected them, for I am the LORD their God and I will answer them.* ***I will signal for them and gather them in****. Surely I will redeem them; they will be as numerous as before. Though I scatter them among*

*the peoples, **yet in distant lands they will remember me. They and their children will survive, and they will return.***" (NIV)

Whatever word the translators use, the picture is clear or should I say the sound is clear. There is a supernatural blast being heralded, reaching the ends of the earth and finding its way into the heart of God's *'treasured possession'* to bring them home. God hasn't forgotten His people. It is the sound of Heaven ~ deep calling unto deep. It is the sound of prophecy, God's *Noble Theme*, being realized.

Up and down the Jordan Rift Valley in Israel, the migratory path of millions of birds marks the way of passage with each changing season. Just like the birds have a homing and migratory instinct, there is a homing instinct awakened in the hearts of the Jewish people by God Almighty as He whistles for them to come home in this hour. Jewish people are being strangely stirred by God's *Noble Theme* to come back to their ancient homeland and ultimately back to Him.

> **Ezekiel 36:23,24** *"...and the nations shall know that I am the LORD," says the Lord GOD, **"when I am hallowed in you before their eyes. For I will take you from among the nations, gather you out of all countries, and bring you into your own land.***"

The return of the Jewish people back to the land of Israel is about God glorifying His Name and honoring His name in all the nations. "*Our Father Who art in Heaven, 'hallowed' by Thy Name.*" Selah!

END TIME PROPHECIES

> **Jeremiah 33:10,11** *"...yet in the towns of Judah and the streets of Jerusalem that are deserted, inhabited by neither men nor animals, there will be heard once more the sounds of joy and gladness..."* (NIV)

The streets of Jerusalem today are filled with the sound of children's laughter and singing. I have witnessed many processions of young families dancing, singing and rejoicing on their way to the Western

Wall to celebrate a bar mitzvah. Father's kissing their sons, mothers beaming with pride, fathers and children dancing circles around the processions. Musicians playing on the streets! It is not uncommon to hear spontaneous joyful songs and dancing in the streets of Jerusalem and particularly at the Western Wall. Joy fills the streets. Jeremiah saw this day with the eye of his spirit. The ingathering of the exiles and the restoration of Israel is one of the most prophesied events in the Old Testament. The Biblical prophets saw this unprecedented return and restoration in the last day!

> **Jeremiah 33:11** *"...there will be heard once more, the voices of the bride and bridegroom..."* (NIV)

The voices of the bride and the bridegroom are resounding once again throughout the land!

> **Isaiah 27:6** *"In days to come Jacob will take root, Israel will bud and blossom and fill the entire world with fruit."* (NIV)

Today, Israel's produce is exported all over the world, a fulfillment of Isaiah's prophecy. Nations of the world are feasting on the bounty of the land. If you live outside the land of Israel, the next time you go to a grocery store or super market and find produce from Israel, rejoice and give thanks because you will be holding Bible prophecy in your hand.

> **Psalm 34:8** *"Taste and see that the LORD is good..."*

Israel is a major exporter of flowers. Israel's *Flower Growers Association* said that Israel exported some 60 million roses, orchids, bonsai trees and other flowers to Europe for Valentine's Day, 2013. Amazing, and all from a Middle Eastern desert climate!

It is interesting to note that no other invading army that trampled the courts and successively conquered the land of Israel over the centuries could ever work the land and cause it to bloom and blossom as the returning sons and daughters of Israel! The land literally has and is responding and coming alive with the return of the Jewish people.

Ezekiel 36:34,35 *"The fields that used to lie empty and desolate in plain view of everyone will again be farmed. And **when I bring you back, people will say, 'This former wasteland is now like the Garden of Eden!** The abandoned and ruined cities now have strong walls and are filled with people!'"*

Amos 9:14 *"I will bring back the captives of My people Israel; They shall build the waste cities and inhabit them; They shall plant vineyards and drink wine from them; **They shall also make gardens and eat fruit from them.**"*

Jerusalem, for one, is an ancient city that has been rebuilt and compacted together in a rich mosaic of old and new, ancient and modern. Modern cities in Israel raised from the ancient ruins bear witness to the prophecies of Ezekiel and Amos.

Amos 9:13,14 *"**New wine will drip from the mountains** and flow from all the hills. They will **plant vineyards and drink their wine**; they will **make gardens and eat their fruit.**"* (NIV)

The mountains in the Galilee region are literally dripping with new wine. The hills are copious with bountiful vineyards. In addition to this, Israel has produced award winning wines in the international arena that rival the best wines in the world! *"O 'sip' and see that the Lord is good!"*

Isaiah 60:11 *"Therefore your gates shall be open continually; they shall not be shut day or night, that men may bring to you the wealth of the Gentiles..."*

The main gateway into the nation of Israel is Ben Gurion Airport. One of its great boasts is that it is open 24/7 receiving the nations that are streaming into the country from all over the world. When the nations come, they are supporting Israel's economy and tourist industry. Based on data released by Independent Media Review Analysis (IMRA), about 3.3 million visitors to Israel arrived in Israel in 2014.
(http://www.imra.org.il/story.php3?id=65953)

Isaiah 55:13 *"Instead of the thorn shall come up the cypress tree, and instead of the brier shall come up the myrtle tree..."*

Many pilgrims, both from Israel and the nations of the world, have planted their roots in the land of Israel by planting trees. This is part of the restoration program in the land through the Jewish National Fund. I have personally planted many trees, on many occasions with groups that I have led to Israel. We have literally removed thorns from our fingers and briars in our path while planting myrtle and cypress trees. Could this be what the prophet Isaiah saw? I believe so.

Isaiah 35:1 *"...the desert shall rejoice and blossom as the rose..."*

I have travelled through and visited the scorching Judean desert and stood in awe when I beheld with my own eyes the desert blossoming as a rose. Israel has developed amazing plantations, orchards, greenhouses and gardens in the desert - a truly remarkable modern day achievement, a sign and wonder of the Lord's doing, all in fulfilment of Bible prophecy. On one occasion, while in Israel, our group sat in the cooling shade of a blossoming almond orchard in the hot Judean desert and fared sumptuously on a picnic lunch simply to sit in the midst of and experience the living Word of God in its fullness and fulfilment. Later that day we visited a kibbutz and saw gardens blooming in the wilderness and amazing Israeli roses blossoming in the desert.

Isaiah 35:6 *"...Water will gush forth in the wilderness and streams in the desert."* (NIV)

Fresh pools of water are now springing up in many places in the desert. It is amazing to see. Around each spring of water, plants grow as an ensign that God is watching over His Word to perform it. The Lord is watering His Word. It is as if with each fresh pool of water and each plant springing up, God is saying, *"Look and see what I the Lord am doing."*

Zephaniah 3:9 *"Then I will purify the language (lips) of the peoples, that all of them may call upon the Name of the Lord and serve Him shoulder to shoulder."* (NIV)

The Hebrew language has been revived after 2,000 years. Imagine 6 million people speaking a language in Israel, and other places in the world for that matter, which no one spoke a little over 100 years ago! This is unprecedented and an amazing Biblical prophecy fulfilled.

These scriptures are only but a few of hundreds that are recorded in the Bible that are being fulfilled in our day! We stand amazed and rejoice in such an hour. As for the prophecies that have not yet been fulfilled, they await their appointed time.

With each passing day, the Word of God is being fulfilled in remarkable ways. The restoration of the land and the people of Israel is clearly an ensign that the prophecies are budding and blossoming. God is *'shakeid,'* watching over His Word to perform it. Lift up your eyes and behold all God is doing at this time in history, His-story, and be ~ ***Stirred by God's Noble Theme!***

CHAPTER FIVE 5

AS YOU DO TO ISRAEL

Obadiah 15 *"For the day of the LORD upon all nations is near;* **As you have done (to Israel), it shall be done to you;** *Your reprisal shall return upon your own head."*

The book of Obadiah is an extremely significant and relevant book for the times in which we live. Through Obadiah's vision, God revealed a great deal about His Covenant land and His Covenant people. Much is to be gleaned from Obadiah, the shortest book in the Old Testament. It is a book of prophetic oracles. Obadiah releases the authoritative judgments of God upon the nation of Edom. *"Who are the Edomites,"* you might ask?

Genesis 36:1 *"Now this is the genealogy of Esau, who is Edom."*

The Edomites were the descendants of Esau. Jacob and Esau were fraternal bothers ~ twins no less! They struggled in their mother's womb. They developed into two nations, Israel and Edom. The Edomites were the cousins of Jacob and settled on the other side of the Jordan River in the land of Edom, south of Moab in the mountainous region of Seir which today is known as Petra. The Edomites fostered and festered an ancient hatred toward Jacob, Israel. In their pride, they also sported a false sense of security. They thought themselves to be impregnable and unconquerable because of their mountainous fortresses.

Obadiah 3 *"The pride of your heart has deceived you, You who dwell in the clefts of the rock, Whose habitation is high; You who say in your heart, 'Who will bring me down to the ground?"*

All forms of pride are rooted in rebellion toward God. It was no mistake that God sent Obadiah, whose name means *'a servant and worshipper of Yahweh,'* to a people who would not serve the God of Israel, bow their knee, nor walk in His ways. They did not worship the God of their forefathers. They did not bless the people of Israel. This same Obadiah is the one who hid the prophets of God, the worshippers of God, in caves during Ahab and Jezebel's malevolent reign.

1 Kings 18:4 *"For so it was, while Jezebel massacred the prophets of the LORD, that Obadiah had taken one hundred prophets and hidden them, fifty to a cave, and had fed them with bread and water."*

Because of the Edomite's pride and rebellion against God, they eventually disappeared into history and ceased to exist as a nation ~ a powerful reminder that pride goes before destruction.

Proverbs 16:18 *"Pride goes before destruction, and a haughty spirit before a fall."*

The Edomites did not come to the aid of their brother Jacob in his time of need and distress. To further worsen the problem, in 586B.C., they aided the Babylonians in seizing and conquering Judah. Obadiah continues his oracle by recounting the transgressions of the Edomites against their brother Jacob.

Obadiah 10-14 *"For violence against your brother Jacob, Shame shall cover you, and you shall be cut off forever. In the day that you stood on the other side—* (some translations say *'stood aloof'* – author's note) *in the day that strangers carried captive his forces, when foreigners entered his gates and cast lots for Jerusalem— Even you were as one of them. "But you should not have gazed on the day of your brother, in the day of his captivity; nor should you have rejoiced over the children of Judah in the day of their destruction; nor should you have* *spoken proudly in the day of distress. You should not have entered the gate of My people in the day of their calamity. Indeed, you should not have gazed on their affliction in the day of their calamity, nor laid hands on their substance in the day of their calamity. You should not have stood at the crossroads to cut off those among them who escaped; nor should you have delivered up those among them who remained in the day of distress."*

1. The Edomites remained *'on the other side'* and did not cross over to help Jacob ~ **The Edomites stood aloof**.

2. Strangers carried captive the forces of Jacob ~ **The Edomites stood aloof**.

3. Foreigners entered the gates of Jerusalem. It was a hostile invasion ~ **The Edomites stood aloof**.

4. Foreigners cast lots for Jerusalem and partitioned God's chosen City. They divided God's covenant land ~ **The Edomites stood aloof**.

After listing these indictments, Obadiah makes a sobering statement.

Obadiah 11 *"...Even you were as one of them."*

"Oh wait," you might be thinking to yourself, *"the Edomites didn't commit those atrocities."* Correct! However, God clearly intimates that standing on the other side, watching, observing and doing nothing is the same as committing the atrocities. That is difficult to comprehend. The Hebrew word for *'aloof'* is *'neged'* (Strong's 5048) which means to stand in front of or in the face of, to observe a thing and do nothing. The Edomites saw. The Edomites observed. The Edomites did nothing. They made a deliberate and conscious choice to *'stand aloof'* and remain on the other side. God said, *"Even you were as one of them."* The consequences were harsh!

Furthermore, Obadiah specifically lists additional transgressions of the Edomites:

1. **Verse 12:** They gazed upon their brother in the day of His captivity and rejoiced over the children of Judah in the day of their destruction.

2. **Verse 12:** They spoke proudly in the day of their brother's distress.

3. **Verse 13:** They entered the gates of God's people in the day of their calamity.

4. **Verse 13:** They gazed on their affliction in the day of their calamity.

5. **Verse 13:** They laid hands on their substance in the day of their calamity.

6. **Verse 14:** They stood at the crossroads to cut off those among them who escaped.

7. **Verse 14:** They delivered up those among them who remained in the day of distress.

Both sins of omission and commission brought the judgment of God.

NATIONS WILL BE JUDGED

Obadiah 15 *"For the day of the LORD upon all the nations is near; as you have done, it shall be done to you; Your reprisal shall return upon your own head."*

Lessons abound from the book of Obadiah. Warnings are pronounced. This is very sobering. Nations will be judged by God's standard alone. He is the Righteous Judge. He has dropped the plumb line of His Word. *"I will bless those who bless Israel, I will curse those who curse you!"* The words of Obadiah echo down the corridors of time, even to this day. The implications and applications of Obadiah's pronouncement are such that God will bless those who are engaged in blessing Israel and will curse those who curse Israel and stand aloof. There is a day of judgment for all nations. That day is near ~ It is the Day of the Lord!

> **Obadiah 15** *"The day of the LORD is near for all nations. As you have done, (to Israel) it will be done to you; your deeds will return upon your own head."*

SCATTERING MY PEOPLE AND DIVIDING MY LAND

> **Joel 3:1-3** *"For behold, in those days and at that time, when I bring back the captives of Judah and Jerusalem, I will also gather all nations, and bring them down to the Valley of Jehoshaphat; and I will enter into judgment with them there on account of **My people, My heritage Israel**, whom **they have scattered** among the nations; They have also **divided up My land**. They have **cast lots for My people**."*

Joel speaks of both a present and a future judgment of nations. While the chapter describes the judgement of God upon the nations that afflicted Judah and Jerusalem during the Babylonian captivity and after their return from exile, the prophetic pronouncement also speaks of future ongoing judgment.

> **Zechariah 12:1-3,9** *"The burden of the word of the LORD against Israel. Thus says the LORD, who stretches out the heavens, lays the foundation of the earth, and forms the spirit of man within him: **"Behold, I will make Jerusalem a cup of drunkenness to all the surrounding peoples**, when they lay siege against Judah and Jerusalem. And it shall happen in that day that **I will make Jerusalem a very heavy stone for all peoples;** all who **would move it away will surely be cut in pieces**, though all nations of the earth are gathered against it. It shall be in that day that **I will seek to destroy all the nations that come against Jerusalem**."*

FACING THE CONSEQUENCES

Bill Koenig, a Washington White House correspondent has authored a book entitled: *Eye to Eye: Facing the Consequences of Dividing Israel*. I recommend his book for a more comprehensive study regarding the consequences of dividing God's Covenant land *(Eye to Eye: ISBN 0-9717347-0-4)*

Bill Koenig is the president of *Koenig's World Watch Daily (http://watch.org)*. *Koenig's Eye View* is the news journal of William Koenig. Since May 7, 2004, Koenig has provided a weekly *'Behind the Scenes'* news report from the White House linked with insider analysis to deliver substantive intelligence relating to news, consequences and prophecy, primarily regarding the U.S.

Bill's book, *Eye to Eye: Facing the Consequences of Dividing Israel*, is very compelling and sobering. Koenig has researched and meticulously chronicled for decades, the United States' administration and their involvement in the *Middle East Peace Process* ~ dividing the 'land for peace'. In Bill's book, he provides undeniable facts and conclusive evidence that indeed the leaders of the United States and the world are on a collision course with the God of Israel when they set out to divide God's Covenant land, Israel. The premise of his book connects the dots, with compelling persuasion. Each time the United States involves itself in the *Middle East Peace Process* to pressure Israel to divide God's Covenant land and/or meets with the Palestinian government regarding the 'two-state solution', a catastrophe ensues within a day or two of the negotiations. This commands every nation's attention and serious examination particularly any nation presently involved in the 'land for peace' plans.

Bill addresses the question: Are each of these major record setting events a mere coincidence or shocking signs that God is actively involved in the affairs of Israel?

- The ten costliest insurance events in U.S. history
- The twelve costliest hurricanes in U.S. history
- The three of the four largest tornado outbreaks in U.S. history
- The two largest terrorism events in U.S. history

When a tragedy or catastrophe following participation in the 'land for peace' process occurs once or twice, one might perhaps write it off as a coincidence. If it happens a few more times, one might raise his eyebrows. But if it happens on multiplied dozens of occasions almost without exception, one needs to pay attention!

With precision and proficiency Bill Koenig relays numerous examples demonstrating that God is indeed watching over His Word. God is also indeed watching over His covenant land. God's warnings to the nations are serious. With dates and times of meetings documented with respect to the United States and Israel and/or the Palestinians to divide God's Covenant land, the ensuing results are clear. *"I will enter into judgement against the nations that seek to divide My land."*

ARIEL SHARON'S DISENGAGEMENT PLAN

The most poignant and striking example of the consequences of pressuring Israel to divide God's Covenant land was evidenced by the Gaza disengagement in August 2005.

Former Israeli Prime Minister Ariel Sharon came under enormous international pressure to give away 'land for peace'. PM Sharon's vision for peace with the Palestinian's became known as the *Disengagement Plan*.

The following are excerpts from Prime Minister Sharon's public addresses at the fourth Herzliya Conference on December 18, 2003. This marked the first presentation of his *Disengagement Plan*.

> *"The State of Israel is committed to the peace process and aspires to reach an agreed resolution of the conflict based upon the vision of US President George Bush. The Disengagement Plan is the only political plan accepted by Israel, the Palestinians, the Americans and a majority of the international community. We are willing to proceed toward its implementation: Two States - Israel and a Palestinian State - living side by side in tranquility, security, and peace. The Road Map is a clear and reasonable plan, and it is therefore possible and imperative*

to implement it. The concept behind this plan is that only security will lead to peace - and in that sequence. Without the achievement of full security - within the framework of which terrorist organizations will be dismantled - it will not be possible to achieve genuine peace, a peace for generations. This is the essence of the Road Map."

"The Israeli disengagement from Gaza, also known as 'Gaza expulsion' and 'Hitnatkut', was the withdrawal of the Israeli army from Gaza, and the dismantling of all Israeli settlements in the Gaza Strip in 2005. Four small settlements in the northern West Bank were also evacuated. The disengagement was proposed by Israeli Prime Minister Ariel Sharon, adopted by the government on June 6, 2004 and enacted in August 2005. Those Israeli citizens who refused to accept government compensation packages and voluntarily vacate their homes prior to the August 15, 2005 deadline, were evicted by Israeli security forces over a period of several days. The eviction of all residents, demolition of the residential buildings and evacuation of associated security personnel from the Gaza Strip was completed by September 12, 2015."

(http://en.wikipedia.org/wiki/Israeli_disengagement_from_Gaza)

Under international pressure, the proposed solution sounded achievable to its advocates. However it contradicted the Word of God. With all due respect to former Prime Minister Ariel Sharon, his road map to peace directly opposed God's Biblical directives. God's covenant land was not to be divided, sold or given away. Ariel Sharon's *Disengagement Plan* was tragically a set-up for failure and in keeping with God's warnings from scripture, invoked the judgments of God.

The dismantling of the Jewish settlements in Gaza and the evacuation of thousands of Israelis, all in the name of peace, was met in the ensuing years with more than 11,000 rockets launched at nearby Israeli communities, villages and cities. This was somewhat of a rude awakening to the nations of the world. Gaza soon deteriorated into a rogue terrorist state! Literally hundreds of underground tunnels from Egypt were constructed to smuggle weapons and arms into Gaza to slaughter, annihilate and destroy the Jewish people. This sounds a little too akin to Haman's decree to slaughter, annihilate and destroy the Jewish people.

> **Esther 7:4** *"For I and my people have been sold for **destruction, and slaughter and annihilation...**"*

On July 8th, 2014, Israel launched a military operation called, *Operation Protective Edge*. The mission was to stop the incessant rocket fire from Gaza. Since the beginning of *Operation Protective Edge*, the IDF uncovered dozens of terrorist tunnels in Gaza leading underground into surrounding Jewish communities. Hamas had invested millions of dollars and other resources in building and operating its massive tunnel network. Every month, Israel, with intent to aide the Palestinian people, transferred construction materials into Gaza intended for civil projects to build infrastructure. The materials were seized by Hamas for tunnel construction. Since January 2014, 4,680 Israeli trucks carrying 181,000 tons of gravel, iron, cement, wood and other supplies have passed through the Kerem Shalom crossing into Gaza. With these supplies, Hamas could have built houses, hospitals, schools and libraries. It could have built infrastructure to improve the quality of life for the residents of Gaza. Instead, it elected to expand its underground terrorist city.

(http://www.idfblog.com/blog/2014/07/31/everything-need-know-hamas-underground-city-terror/)

PRIME MINISTER BENJAMIN NETANYAHU

Prime Minister Benjamin Netanyahu has stated:

> *"If the Arabs were to put down their arms there would be no more war. The truth is that if Israel were to put down its arms there would be no more Israel."*

(http://en.wikiquote.org/wiki/Benjamin_Netanyahu)

Golda Meir, a former prime minister of Israel stated, *"Peace will come when the Arabs will love their children more than they hate us."*

PROPHETIC PARALLELS: GAZA DISENGAGEMENT AND KATRINA

Hurricane Katrina was one of the deadliest hurricanes ever to hit the United States. An estimated 1,836 people died in the hurricane and the flooding that followed in late August 2005, and millions of others were left homeless along the Gulf Coast and in New Orleans, which experienced the highest death toll. Officials at the *National Oceanic and Atmospheric Administration* stated Katrina was the most destructive storm to strike the United States. Total property damage from Katrina was estimated at $81 billion, which was nearly triple the damage inflicted by Hurricane Andrew in 1992.

(http://www.livescience.com/22522-hurricane-katrina-facts.html)

Some of the parallels between the Gaza Disengagement and Hurricane Katrina are eerily evident. Katrina caused untold damage affecting Louisiana, Mississippi & Alabama and laid waste the City of New Orleans. Hundreds of thousands of US citizens were evacuated from their homes. As the United States did to Israel, so God did to the United States in direct proportion.

AS YOU DO TO ISRAEL

The following statistics are extracted from Bill Koenig's book Eye to Eye, page 161.

Date	Action	Date	Catastrophe
15.08.2005	• 63,000 Israeli soldiers and police delivered eviction notices to Israeli settlers living in Gaza and northern Samaria.	23.08.2005	**Hurricane Katrina:** Largest disaster in U.S. history affected Louisiana, Mississippi & Alabama; devastated New Orleans; forced 1 million people from their homes; 225,000 homes were destroyed; 473,000 people without work; estimated cost to insurers: $40.4 billion; U.S. Government will spend $112- $200 billion.
15.08.2005 to 23.08.2005	• With tears and multiple protests, 9,000 Israeli settlers completely evacuated 25 communities; most left voluntarily, but many were forcibly removed by Israeli troops; 3,000 homes were destroyed.		
17.08.2005	• Israeli PM Ariel Sharon authorized mandatory evacuation of residents refusing to leave Gaza.		
17.08.2005	• U.S. Secretary of State Condoleezza Rice said evacuation "cannot be Gaza only."		
19.08.2005	• In Gaza, U.S. Asst. Sec. of State David Welsh said Gaza pullout would re-energize "Road Map" peace plan.		
22.08.2005	• Pres. Bush said, "We'll continue working for the day when the map of the Middle East shows two democratic states, Israel and Palestine, living side-by-side in peace and security."		
22.08.2005	• Pres. Bush said, "My vision, my hope, is that one day we'll see two states – two democratic states – living side-by-side in peace."		

Could it be that Hurricane Katrina was a judgment from God for the Gaza disengagement?

Could it be that the millions of U.S. citizens who experienced forced evacuation from their homes was a 'sowing and reaping' consequence to Israel's forced unilateral evacuation from Gaza?

Could it be that U.S. citizens driven away from their homes in buses was a cause and effect related to Israeli citizens of Gaza driven away from their homes in buses?

Could it be that the destruction of U.S. homes and businesses by Katrina was linked to the destruction of Israeli homes and businesses in Gaza?

Could it be that American News Agencies that openly dubbed those displaced from their homes as 'refugees' was associated to the Israeli refugees that were forced out of their homes in Gaza?

Could it be that the massive upturned graves reported by the U.S. media had its root connection to the massive upturned graves in Gaza?

Could it be that the financial collateral damage experienced in the Gulf refineries was linked to the inevitable enormous economic loss in Gaza?

Could it be that the devastation in the Gulf Sea Port was a consequence of the forced evacuation of one of Israel's greatest ports of export at Gaza?

Could it be that Katrina was a retribution as in Obadiah 15, *"As you have done to Israel, it shall be done to you?"*

Could it be that the answer to all of these questions and countless other parallels be a resounding, *'Yes?'*

COMMENTS ON THE GAZA DISENGAGEMENT GAZA AND KATRINA: A TERRIBLE CONNECTION

FREEMAN CENTER BROADCAST September 5, 2005

http://www.jewishawareness.org/gaza-and-katrina-a-terrible-connection/

Bernard J. Shapiro is the Executive Director of the Freeman Center for Strategic Studies. Shapiro states:

"We have witnessed two great tragedies in the last few weeks. One, the expulsion of Jews from Gaza, was a man-made catastrophe. In fact, it was a crime against the Jewish People perpetuated by the Jewish government of Israeli PM Ariel Sharon. Sharon was not alone in this criminal act. The United States, through its State Department and President George Bush aided and abetted this act against G-d's Covenant with Abraham."

"The second tragedy appears to be a natural phenomenon. Sometimes the wrong that men do seems to go unpunished. Sometimes the consequences are quick and furious. I have received many dozens of letters from both Christian Zionists and religious Jews telling me that they feel that Katrina was retribution for Gaza. The people of New Orleans and the Gulf Coast of Mississippi were not guilty of the crimes against the Jews of Gaza. Unfortunately the Scales of Justice do not work with perfect human logic. They are subject to a divine purpose not always apparent to us. Jewish history is filled with nations who persecuted us and then fell and disappeared into the dustbin of history."

"The Egyptians, the Babylonians, the Assyrians, the Persians, the Greeks and the Romans persecuted us and destroyed our Temples – and they are gone; other peoples have sprung up high and mighty and now they have vanished. In the 20th Century, we witnessed the German attempt to exterminate us and the Soviet Communist persecution. Where are they now? Gone! In 1948 and many times since the Arabs have tried to destroy

> *Israel. They never succeeded, but now they are aided by the Israeli government of Sharon and the American government of Bush."*

Jan Willem van der Hoeven, Director International Christian Zionist Center, had this to say about the connection of Katrina and Gaza:

> *"God's answer was shocking in its severity. The same scenes the whole world had been watching just barely a week before were now again before our eyes, this time however not in Israel's Gush Katif, but in Louisiana's New Orleans and other parts of the United States: People driven from their homes – put in buses to be brought to hotels or other places of assembling – just as a few days ago, under pressure and to words of praise from President Bush and his Secretary of State, Israelis had been cruelly uprooted from their own homes and livelihood and put on buses. Who can deny the parallel and the finger of G-d in all this, of Him Who says through His Word that 'He who touches you, Israel, touches the apple of His Eye?"*

Gershon Salomon of the Temple Mount Faithful spoke in Houston to a large crowd of over 200 Christian Zionists and a few Jews. When he mentioned the connection between Gaza and Katrina, there was loud applause. This was a group of people who voted for Bush and are among the most patriotic Americans but they saw G-d's hand in the disaster in New Orleans. I don't believe that the people who draw this connection are exploitative or opportunistic. They are quite sincere and G-d fearing people.

> *"I am a political analyst and not a religious scholar. But I see the Hand of G-d in recent events and it brings trembling to my soul. I have always believed in the importance of Israel in the fulfillment of Biblical prophecy. Over the past 57 years, I have seen many miracles in the Land of Israel. The power of the Jews when reunited with the Land of Israel was magnified greatly. In strictly military terms, its power was much greater than the sum of its arms and men. In intellectual and economic terms, we have all witnessed miracles from Israel."*

*"I believe the forced expulsion of the Jews from Gaza and N. Shomron has upset the Holy biblical command to "settle the Land." This retreat from the principles of Zionism has severe consequences for all that were involved in that policy. It may not be politically correct to say it, but we are only beginning to witness the full extent of the Wrath of the Almighty. History has proven over and over again that "He who blesses Israel will be blessed and he who curses Israel will be cursed." Another important lesson of history enunciated by Santayana is: Those who fail to learn from history, are condemned to repeat it. Jews as well as the nations of the world frequently failed to learn these lessons. The post-Zionist leadership of Israel had best begin to educate themselves about the consequences of their actions. Of course, this is equally true of the nations of the world. It is my fond hope that the future will be better for all concerned as **TRUTH** begins to penetrate the darkness."*

CATASTROPHIC CONNECTIONS

It is a tragic reality that Bill Koenig's book *Eye to Eye* is crammed with examples of catastrophic consequences following U.S. policy and political engagement pressuring Israel to divide its Covenant land. United States is not the only country that has suffered the consequences. Bill's investigative research is thorough and exhaustive! Following are some examples from *Eye to Eye: Facing the Consequences of Dividing Israel* and related postings from Koenig's World Watch Daily *(http://watch.org)*

Date	Action	Date	Catastrophe
18.10.1991	Secretary of State James A. Baker III states that President George W. Bush and Soviet President Mikhail Gorbachev were inviting the Arab nations and the Palestinians to attend a Middle East Peace Conference to be held in Madrid on October 30th, 1991.	20.10.1991	**Oakland Fire:** Most costly and worst fire in terms of loss of life and property since the great San Francisco earthquake and fire in 1906 in U.S. It occurred within 48 hours of the Bush Administration's announcement of the Madrid 'land for peace' Conference. Magnitude and scope of 'Tunnel Fires' was beyond anything firefighters have ever experienced.
30.10.1991	Madrid Peace Conference. Convened by U.S and former Soviet Union. Pres. Bush made it clear to the Israelis that America did not accept the permanent occupation of the West Bank and Gaza.	31.10.1991	**The Perfect Storm:** Extremely rare weather patterns, created monster storm with record breaking ocean waves crashing into the east coast of USA into the Carolinas causing heavy damage to Pres. Bush's family home in Maine. Front page of USA Today Newspaper reported the two events Dividing the Land & Catastrophe. $200 million damage.
24.08.1992	Bi-Lateral Peace Talks in Washington D.C.	24.08.1992	**Hurricane Andrew:** Category five storm with winds at 177 mph. hitting Florida. It became the worst natural disaster ever to hit America. 180,000 homeless in Florida and 25,000 in Louisiana. Front page of New York Times and USA Today contained adjacent headlines of Hurricane Andrew and reconvened Middle East Peace Talks. Damage was estimated as high as $30 billion.
16.01.1994	U.S. President Bill Clinton and President Hafez al-Assad of the Syrian Arab Republic made statements at joint news conference regarding Peace talks pressuring Israel to end its 'Israeli Occupation' and give up its covenant land.	17.01.1994	**Northridge Earthquake:** 6.9 earthquake rocked southern California. Second most destructive natural disaster to hit America. (Second to Hurricane Andrew) Damage was estimated at $15 billion.
02.03.1997	President Clinton invites Palestinian leader Yasser Arafat to the White House to discuss "problem" with Jerusalem. Clinton and Arafat release statement criticizing Israel.	02.03.1997	**Mississippi & Ohio Valley flooding and tornados:** 67 dead (26 in Arkansas); winds up to 207-260 mph & tornadoes brought heavy rains, flooding; $1 billion. Pres. Clinton's home state of Arkansas was devastated by tornados.

As You do to Israel

Date	Action	Date	Catastrophe
24.09.1998	U.S. President Bill Clinton announced he was going to meet with Yasser Arafat and Benjamin Netanyahu when they came to New York City to address the United Nations. Purpose of meeting was to discuss the stalled peace plan in which Israel was to give away 13% of its covenant land. On Sept. 28 Clinton, Arafat and Netanyahu met at the White House.	24.09.1998 to 28.09.1998	**Hurricane Georges:** Hits Gulf Coast. Killer storm zeros in on Key West. $6.5 billion dollar damages/cost.
11.09.2001	According to *The Washington Post*, for 17 days prior to 9-11 terror events, President Bush – with the encouragement and involvement of Secretary Powell and the U.S. Ambassador to Israel, Daniel Kurtzer, and in cooperation with the Saudis – was working on the most comprehensive plan and message ever to be offered about Israel's covenant land by an American president. Bush and his top officials had completed a majority of their work on September 10th. Secretary Powell was to present the plan to the United Nations General Assembly on September 24, 2001.	11.09.2001	**911 Terrorist Attack on World Trade Centre and Pentagon:** Greatest attack ever on American soil left nearly 3,000 dead. 100's of billions of dollars in damages/costs.
04.12.2002	• PM Ariel Sharon accepted in principle Road Map envisioning independent Palestinian State.	05.12.2002	**Worst Ice Storm in History of North and South Caroline:** 2 million homes and businesses without power. 24 killed.
05.12.2002	• Bush commemorated end of Ramadan at Islamic Centre in DC, saying it "commemorates the revelation of God's word in the Holy Koran to the prophet Mohamad."		
31.01.2003	Secretary Powell said President Bush would become more involved in Israeli-Palestinian talks with goal of creating a Palestinian state in Israel by 2005.	01.02.2003	**Space Shuttle Columbia:** Broke up over 'Palestine' Texas, upon entry into earth's atmosphere; all 7 astronauts including first Israeli (on space mission) and 3 Christians, died.

Stirred by a Noble Theme

Date	Action	Date	Catastrophe
15.07.2003	Last days of meetings in D.C. between Palestinian officials and members of Congress & Bush Administration officials discussing.	15.07.2003	**Hurricane Claudette:** Hits Texas, President Bush's home state. $100 million damages/cost.
09.2004	Bush administration kept up pressure on Israel to leave 'unauthorized settlements.'	03.09.2004	**Hurricane Ivan:** Hits Florida and Alabama – 2 million advised to evacuate their homes. $6 billion dollar cost to insurers.
2008	Major events that coincided with US Secretary of State Condoleezza Rice's trip to Israel. Record-setting events that corresponded with President George W. Bush and/or Secretary of State Rice's peace efforts in 2008.	2008	• Southern California experienced an earthquake near Chino Hills on July 29, the largest since the 1994 Northridge earthquake. • One of the largest and costliest floods in U.S. history. • In the year 2008 there was a total of 2,127 tornadoes through November (NOAA), the most-ever recorded in one year. • Hurricane Dolly slammed into South Texas on July 23, the day Barack Obama was in Jerusalem committing to a Palestinian state and the splitting of Jerusalem.
15.12.2010	Australia's Foreign Minister Kevin Rudd wrapped up a visit to the Middle East by telling Israel it should allow UN inspectors into its nuclear facilities and to join Nuclear Non-Proliferation Treaty (NPT). Australia backs refugees and Palestinian State. Australia will give $18 million over three years.		**Australia Flood:** "Disaster of Biblical Proportions." Floods Worst Disaster In Australian History in Kevin Rudd's hometown of West End, a suburb of Brisbane, was flooded.
11.03.2010 11.01.2011 10.02.2011	• The Government of Japan deplores decisions of Israel to construct housing in E. Jerusalem and in the West Bank. • Japan condemns the demolishing of a part of the Shepherd's Hotel in East Jerusalem with a view to constructing new housing units for Jewish people. • The Government of Japan is concerned about the Jerusalem municipal planning committee's approval of a plan to build housing units for Jewish people in the Sheikh Jarrah of East Jerusalem.		**Japan Tsunami:** Quake moved Japan coast 8 feet; shifted Earth's axis by 4 inches. The Japan earthquake was the fourth most powerful ever recorded with a magnitude of 9.1 Biggest crisis Japan has faced since the end of World War Two.
04.03.2012	U.S. Prime Minister Barak Obama addresses AIPAC and calls for 1967 borders with land swaps.		**50 Major Tornadoes:** Strike Joplin, MO and Minneapolis.

Of interest, Bill Koenig reveals further connections between the *'Divide the Land'* peace talks and personal calamities that befell presidents and/or government leaders. Some of the possible consequences in opposing God's 'one-state solution' that he emphasized were personal scandals, party scandals, perjury, obstruction of justice, impeachment, personal loss of property, presidents' home states devastated, to name a few. As well, political polls indicated a decline of popularity with presidents and heads of state followed by a subsequent political decline of majority governments.

Some might say that the above conclusions are not scientifically substantiated and therefore its conclusions cannot be accepted as accurate. Perhaps! The measure by which one observes and makes conclusions about the consequences of dividing God's Covenant land cannot come from the realm of science. Conclusions are rooted in the veracity of the enduring Word of God ~ the only plumb line! God is watching over His Word to perform it. Who could deny the parallels?

> **Obadiah 15** *"For the day of the LORD upon all the nations is near; **As you have done, (to Israel) it shall be done to you;** Your reprisal shall return upon your own head."*
>
> **Joel 3:1-3** *"For behold, in those days and at that time, when I bring back the captives of Judah and Jerusalem, I will also gather all nations, and bring them down to the Valley of Jehoshaphat; And **I will enter into judgment with them there on account of My people, My heritage Israel, whom they have scattered among the nations; They have also divided up My land.** They have **cast lots for My people.**"*
>
> **Zechariah 12:2,3** *"I am going to make **Jerusalem a cup that sends all the surrounding peoples reeling. Judah will be besieged as well as Jerusalem.** On that day when all the nations of the earth are gathered against her, I will make Jerusalem an immovable rock for all the nations. **All who try to move it will injure themselves.**"* (NIV)
>
> **Zechariah 12:9** *"It shall be in that day that I will seek to destroy all the nations that come against Jerusalem."*

> On the mountains of Israel, stand in awe,
> Behold with your eyes all that Abraham saw.
> God gave unto him and all of his seed,
> The land spread before him, both title and deed.
>
> God bestowed *'His Land'* with firm resolution,
> He never intended a 'two-state solution!'
> Hear the voice of the prophets when they spoke in accord,
> For what they proclaimed was the Word of the Lord!
>
> Consider God's warnings and don't think it odd,
> Be still, O you nations, and know He is God.
> His intention is clear, His Word is still true,
> As you do unto Israel, He'll do unto you!

God's 'one-state solution' remains ~ ***His Noble Theme!***

CHAPTER SIX

ISRAEL'S PEACE PARTNERS

Exodus 34:15 *"Be careful not to make a treaty with those who live in the land…"*

Several times throughout scripture God specifically instructed the people of Israel not to make a treaty, nor an alliance nor a covenant with those who live in the land who worshipped foreign gods.

God stated,

Exodus 34:15 *"…for when they prostitute themselves to their gods and sacrifice to them, they will invite you and you will eat their sacrifices."*

The worship of other Gods was strictly forbidden. Relationship with the God of Israel and worship of the Almighty was paramount of all the commandments given to Moses on Mount Sinai. The first four commandments deal with Israel's relationship with God.

Exodus 20:1-8 *"And God spoke all these words, saying: "I am the LORD your God, who brought you out of the land of Egypt, out of the house of bondage. "**You shall** have no other gods before Me. "**You shall not** make for yourself a carved image—any likeness of anything that is in heaven above, or that is in the earth beneath, or that is in the water under the earth; you shall not bow down to them nor serve them. For I, the LORD your God, am a jealous God, visiting the iniquity of the fathers upon the children* *to the third and fourth generations of those who hate Me, but showing mercy to thousands, to those who love Me and keep My commandments.* **You shall not** *take the name of the LORD your God in vain, for the LORD will not hold him guiltless who takes His name in vain.* **Remember** *the Sabbath day, to keep it holy."*

God was gracious to the foreigners and the strangers who dwelt among the people of Israel. He made abundant provision for them to live in the land but always under His benevolent sovereign reign as clearly indicated in the Torah, given to Moses and administered through God's chosen people.

> **Leviticus 19:34** *"The stranger who dwells among you shall be to you as one born among you, and you shall love him as yourself; for you were strangers in the land of Egypt: I am the LORD your God."*

> **Deuteronomy 10:19** *"Therefore love the stranger, for you were strangers in the land of Egypt."*

> **Deuteronomy 26:19** *"He has declared that he will set you in praise, fame and honor high above all the nations he has made and that you will be a people holy to the LORD your God, as he promised that you may be a holy people to the LORD your God, just as He has spoken."* (NIV)

God clearly set the boundaries for the nation of Israel and defined its borders as we read in Exodus 23:31-33. After defining the boundaries, God instructed the Israelites not to make a treaty with the people in the land. Israel's covenant was with God who would make every provision for their safety and wellbeing.

> **Exodus 23:31-33** *"And I will set your bounds from the Red Sea to the sea, Philistia, and from the desert to the River. For I will deliver the inhabitants of the land into your hand, and you shall drive them out before you.* **You shall make no covenant with them**, *nor with their gods. They shall not dwell in your land, lest they make you sin against Me. For if you serve their gods, it will surely be a snare to you."*

> **Exodus 34:12-15** *"**Be careful not to make a treaty** with those who live in the land where you are going, or they will be a snare among you. Break down their altars, smash their sacred stones and cut down their Asherah poles. Do not worship any other god, for the LORD, whose name is Jealous, is a jealous God. **"Be careful not to make a treaty** with those who live in the land; for when they prostitute themselves to their gods and sacrifice to them, they will invite you and you will eat their sacrifices."* (NIV)

In addition, the land was not to be divided nor sold. Since the 2003 road map for peace, the current outline for a Palestinian–Israeli peace agreement has been a 'two-state solution'.
(http://en.wikipedia.org/wiki/Israeli%E2%80%93Palestinian_peace_process)

The end result of a 'two-state solution' no matter how the land is carved up, would be in contradiction to the Word of God. The 'two-state solution' is not, nor will it ever be God's solution. Israel is not to give up her God given inheritance. God is jealous over His covenant land and covenant people. God's will as stated in the Bible is a 'one-state solution!'

PALESTINIAN PARTNERS

The Palestinian National Authority is a self-governing body. Following elections in 2006 and the subsequent Gaza conflict between the Fatah and Hamas parties, its authority had extended only as far as the West Bank. The Palestinian Authority, led by the Fatah Party, has continued to oversee the Palestinian territories in the West Bank, while the Hamas government has continued to control the Gaza Strip.

Mahmoud Abbas, also known as Abu Mazen, currently (2016) serves as prime minister of the Palestinian Authority.
(http://www.britannica.com/EBchecked/topic/906746/Mahmoud-Abbas)

Hamas is one of the two major political parties of Gaza, its counterpart being Fatah, currently the leader of the Palestinian Authority. In 2006, Hamas won the Palestinian legislative election. A

year later, Fatah leaders led a coup against Hamas and effectively split Palestine between the West Bank and Gaza.
(http://www.ibtimes.com/what-difference-between-isis-hamas-1653782)

Canada currently lists Hamas as one of 55 terrorist entities.
(http://www.publicsafety.gc.ca/cnt/ntnl-scrt/cntr-trrrsm/lstd-ntts/crrnt-lstd-ntts-eng.aspx#2001)

It is important to note that Israel's peace partner, the Palestinian Authority, does not believe in Israel's right to exist. The Palestinian Authority do not support a 'two-state solution'. They are coveting the destruction of Israel and *one-state* for one people, the Palestinian people.

Reported on i24News.TV headline, November 29, 2014, Prime Minister Mahmoud Abbas has stated, *"Palestinians will never recognize Israel as Jewish state."*
(http://www.i24news.tv/en/news/israel/diplomacy-defense/52766-141129-abbas-threatens-to-halt-security-cooperation-with-israel-if-talks-remain-stalled)

The Hamas Covenant 1988 - The Covenant of the Islamic Resistance Movement, *"Israel will exist and will continue to exist until Islam will obliterate it, just as it obliterated others before it."*
(http://avalon.law.yale.edu/20th_century/hamas.asp)

Part of the Fatah Constitution under Article 12 calls for the:

> *"Complete liberation of Palestine, and the eradication of Zionist economic, political, military and cultural existence."*
> *(https://www.mythsandfacts.org/conflict/statute-treaties/all.htm)*

Since the Oslo Peace Accord, the Camp David Peace Talks, the Road Map to Peace and the ongoing, often stalled subsequent 'land for peace' *negotiations* to resolve the conflict, peace has been elusive.

In the eyes of many, it is incomprehensible that Israel be expected to sit at a bargaining table and negotiate with a people who deny Israel's right to exist and in addition call for Israel's destruction.

May the eyes of all nations pressuring Israel to divide its God given covenant land and the eyes of Israel's peace partners be enlightened to Heaven's noble plan and be ~ ***Stirred by God's Noble Theme!***

CHAPTER SEVEN

O ISRAEL, WE STAND ON GUARD FOR THEE

"God keep our land glorious and free!
O Canada, we stand on guard for thee!"

(Excerpt from Canada's National Anthem)

Canada's national anthem is a proclamation, a prayer and a pledge.

Each time Canada's national anthem is sung, a choir of voices extols the beauty and greatness of our glorious land *"the true north strong and free."*

Every time our national anthem is sung, a chorus of voices rises to implore the protective hand of the Almighty, *"God keep our land glorious and free."*

Whenever our national anthem is sung, a concert of voices rises in pledge to stand on guard, *"O Canada, we stand on guard for thee."*

The prayer and the pledge are one and the same: to protect, to guard, to keep, to watch over and to preserve!

I have a deep and profound love for Canada, my home and native land. There is hardly ever a time when I sing our national anthem that my heart is not filled with an enduring national pride and deep gratitude to God for my country. My eyes well up. I sing our national anthem with a deliberate and sincere focus on the proclamation, the prayer and the pledge. I am grateful to live in a nation that is one of the most blessed nations on earth.

Psalm 33:12 *"Blessed is the nation whose God is the LORD..."*

THE DOMINION OF CANADA

Canada was founded on Biblical values, righteous roots and Christian foundations. This bedrock is the core on which our Canadian Fathers of Confederation built our nation.

Life in the Atlantic Provinces in the 1800's rested firmly on the Christian foundations laid in the earliest days of European settlement and augmented through the evangelistic efforts of many churches in the province. One product of this Christian heritage was Sir Samuel Leonard Tilley, (May 8, 1818 – June 25, 1896), Premier of New Brunswick at the time of Confederation and a Father of Confederation.

His direct contribution to Canada's Christian heritage is truly national in scope. From Tilley came both Canada's official motto and our nation's unique title: *"The Dominion of Canada."*

Both the term *"Dominion"* and the motto *"A mari usque ad mare,"* are taken from:

Psalm 72:8 *"He shall have dominion also from sea to sea, and from the river unto the ends of the earth."*

Sir Samuel Leonard Tilley's son tells of his father's contribution:

"I have heard my father state how he came to suggest it at the B.N.A. Conference. When the fathers of Confederation were assembled discussing the terms and conditions of Confederation and the drafting of the British North America Act, there had been considerable discussion the day before and many suggestions as to what the new United Canada should be called, and no conclusion had been reached. The discussion on the name stood over until the next day. The next morning, as

was Sir Leonard's custom, he read a chapter from the Bible, and that particular morning he read **Psalm 72:8 'He shall have dominion also from sea to sea.'** When reading verse 8 of said Psalm, the thought occurred to him, what a splendid name to give Canada... the 'Dominion of Canada.' When he went back to the sitting of the convention that morning, he suggested the word 'Dominion,' which was agreed to, and Canada was called 'Dominion of Canada.' The motto represents Tilley's belief, obviously shared by many of Canada's founding fathers, that God should have His rightful place in the new country, the "Dominion of Canada."
(http://www.sermonindex.net/modules/newbb/viewtopic.php?topic_id=36235&forum=35&4)

A fascinating incident transpired on May 24th, 2006 in our nation's capital, Ottawa. Time stood still as the clock on the Peace Tower, of the Centre Block of the Parliament Buildings, stopped for the very first time in Canadian history. The headline in CBC News was published rather humorously, *"Tourists ticked off after Peace Tower clock stops."*

It was remarkable that the clock stopped precisely at 7:28 in the morning. 7-2-8! Etched in stone immediately below the face of the clock on the Peace Tower is Psalm 72:8, the very Psalm adopted as Canada's official motto!

> 1. Facing east, from **Psalm 72:8** *"He shall have dominion from sea to sea."*
>
> 2. Facing south, **Psalm 72:1**, *"Give the King thy judgements and the King's son thy righteousness."*
>
> 3. Facing west, **Proverbs 29:18** *"Where there is no vision, the people perish."*

Many saw this as the invisible hand of God stopping the hands of time on the Peace Tower clock to make a profound and prophetic statement in our nation. I believe God used that 'moment' to proclaim as in Psalm 72:8 that He indeed has dominion from sea to sea and from the river to the ends of the earth.

Psalm 72:1 *"Give the King thy judgements and the King's son thy righteousness,"* is a prayer attributed to King David beseeching His God for wisdom and discernment for himself and his son, Solomon, to rule and reign over the people of Israel. At the time of the construction of the Peace Tower in the centre block of Parliament Hill, this verse must have been engraved with like-intent that all forthcoming Prime Ministers and their successive governments might be endowed with divine wisdom from above to implement righteous judgement, wisdom and justice over the Dominion of Canada.

Proverbs 29:18 *"Where there is no vision, the people perish,"* is a profoundly significant scripture etched on the west side of the Peace Tower. *"Blessed is the nation whose God is the Lord,"* aligns with God's vision for a nation. Part of God's vision is to bless the covenant people and the covenant land of Israel. Conversely, God help the nation that implements a vision that is contrary to God's vision, purposes and Noble Theme.

Today, thousands of Christians in Canada stand as watchmen embracing the faith of our forefathers and standing on guard, declaring God's sovereignty, praying for our leaders and those in authority in Canada.

> **1 Timothy 2:1,2** *"I urge, then, first of all, that requests, prayers, intercession and thanksgiving be made for everyone – for kings and all those in authority, that we may live peaceful and quiet lives in all godliness and holiness."* (NIV)

"God keep our land glorious and free!"

O ISRAEL, WE STAND ON GUARD FOR THEE

At the core of Canada's Christian heritage is a faith that is derived from the Bible, from the land of Israel. All Christians owe a debt of profound gratitude to the Jewish People and the nation of Israel. The Jewish roots of our Christian faith have their origin in the Bible. We are grateful for the Word of God, the patriarchs, the prophets, the covenants, the promises and most importantly, Jesus Christ, the Jewish Messiah.

To stand on guard for Canada is to stand on guard for Israel. There is a deep spiritual connection. The roots of our nation's Biblical foundations reach all the way to Israel. God has an abiding and everlasting love for the Jewish people and so Christians ought also to possess that same love.

At a grassroots level, Canada's support for Israel is strong. Jewish and Christian groups travel to Israel in record breaking numbers to show their support, solidarity and love for Israel.

Many Canadian Christian organizations are committed to fulfilling the Biblical mandate to bless, support, serve, comfort and pray for Israel demonstrating God's love and mercy through practical deeds. Many participate in assisting with the enterprise and efforts of *aliyah*, the return of the Jewish people to their homeland. Many promote education and advocacy in light of the defamatory campaigns to boycott, delegitimize, demonize, divest and sponsor sanctions against Israel.

CANADA ~ ISRAEL RELATIONS

Canada recognized the newly established State of Israel in 1948 and the two countries established formal diplomatic relations on May 11, 1949.

Canada and Israel enjoy a steadfast friendship based on shared values, including democracy. Prime Minster Stephen Harper served as Prime Minister in Canada from 2006 – 2015. While leading our nation, he consistently engaged a pro-Israel stance. Canada emerged on the world scene as one of Israel's staunchest and most reliable friends and allies. Prime Minister Harper's pro-Israel support was and still is commendable. Prime Minister Harper stated on numerous occasions, *"Canada's support for Israel is unwavering."*

Posted on the Embassy of Canada to Israel website is the following statement:

> *"Canada and Israel have strong, multidimensional **bilateral relations** marked by close political, economic, social and cultural ties. Support for Israel, especially its right to live in peace and security with its neighbours, has been at the core of Canada's Middle East policy since 1948. The relationship has been strengthened in recent years as evidenced by increased cooperation in several areas including public security, defense, trade and investment, and the increased frequency of ministerial visits. Canada and Israel marked 60 years of diplomatic relations on May 11, 2009. On this occasion, Prime Minister Stephen Harper stated: "At the heart of relations between Canada and Israel is the dynamism of our shared communities. We look forward to the next 60 years and beyond."*
>
> *(http://www.canadainternational.gc.ca/israel/bilateral_relations_bilaterales/index.aspx?lang=eng)*

THROUGH FIRE AND WATER

On January 20, 2014, Prime Minister Stephen Harper addressed the Israeli Knesset and spoke boldly in defense of Israel. He spoke of Canada-Israel longstanding ties and stated that Canada and Israel share the same values. Following are a few excerpts from his speech:

> *"I believe the story of Israel is a great example to the world. It is a story, essentially, of a people whose response to suffering has been to move beyond resentment and build a most extraordinary society - a vibrant democracy, a freedom-loving country. Israelis have taken the collective memory of death and persecution to build an optimistic, forward-looking society - one that so values life it will sometimes release 1,000 criminals and terrorists to save one of its own. In the democratic family of nations, Israel*

represents values that our government takes as articles of faith and principles to drive our own national life. And therefore, **through fire and water, Canada will stand with Israel."**

"First, Canada finds it deplorable that some in the international community still question the legitimacy of the existence of the State of Israel. ***Our view that Israel's right to exist as a Jewish state is absolute and non-negotiable.****"*

"In the world of diplomacy, with one solitary Jewish state and scores of others, it is all too easy to 'go along to get along' and single out Israel. But such going along to get along is not a balanced approach, nor is it a sophisticated one. It is just, quite simply, weak and wrong."

See more at: *(http://daily.pm.gc.ca/en/content/canada-world/why-canada-stands-israel#sthash.axOcL7ny.dpuf)*

Canada has been a strong voice defending Israel's security challenges. Canada has often been the lone voice in the global arena that took a courageously bold moral stand when other nations sought to single out Israel for criticism or delegitimization.

CANADA IS UNEQUIVOCALLY BEHIND ISRAEL

Following relentless rocket and missile fire from Gaza to Israel, on July 8, 2014, the Israeli Defense Force initiated *Operation Protective Edge*. On the 10th day of the operation, after continued terrorist assaults on Israel from land, air and sea, the IDF commenced the ground phase of the operation.

On July 13, 2014, Prime Minister Stephen Harper's office released a statement with regards to *Operation Protective Edge*. Our government took a principled stand in supporting the Israeli operation and Israel's right to defend itself against terrorist attacks.

"Prime Minister Stephen Harper today issued the following statement in response to the situation in Israel: "The indiscriminate rocket attacks from Gaza on Israel are terrorist acts for which there is no justification. It is evident that Hamas is deliberately using human shields to further terror in the region. "Failure by the international community to condemn these reprehensible actions would encourage these terrorists to continue their appalling actions. Canada calls on its allies and partners to recognize that these terrorist acts are unacceptable and that solidarity with Israel is the best way of stopping the conflict. "**Canada is unequivocally behind Israel. We support its right to defend itself, by itself, against these terror attacks**, and urge Hamas to immediately cease their indiscriminate attacks on innocent Israeli civilians. "Canada reiterates its call for the Palestinian government to disarm Hamas and other Palestinian terrorist groups operating in Gaza, including the Iranian proxy, Palestinian Islamic Jihad."

(http://pm.gc.ca/eng/news/2014/07/13/statement-prime-minister-canada-response-situation-israel#sthash.D9RapvsV.dpuf)

WE STAND SHOULDER-TO-SHOULDER WITH ISRAEL

At his meeting with President Reuven Rivlin on Sunday, January 18, 2015, the then Canadian Foreign Affairs Minister John Baird said that *"terrorism is the struggle of our generation,"* and added that, *"unfortunately the State of Israel is too often on the front line of attack."* Minister Baird assured Rivlin that Canada does not just stand behind Israel but shoulder-to-shoulder with Israel. *(Jerusalem Post: January 18, 2015)*

"States have not just a right but an obligation to defend their citizens," he said in relation to the controversy surrounding the decision by the prosecutor of the International Criminal Court in the Hague to open an inquiry as to whether Israel should be investigated for war crimes.

Minister Baird declared,

> "Israel has one hand firmly tied behind its back and we will not allow the international community to tie the other hand."

Minister Baird said,

> "Israel and Canada share the same values, which has made our relationship rock solid. In Canada, had you had 10,000 rockets fired at civilian targets, the Canadian people would have had one simple expectation from their government - to make it stop. States have not just the right, but the obligation to protect their people."

> (http://mfa.gov.il/MFA/PressRoom/2015/Pages/President-Rivlin-meets-with-Canadian-FM-Baird--18-Jan-2015.aspx)

OTTAWA PROTOCOL TO COMBAT ANTI-SEMITISM

Canada leads the way in fighting anti-Semitism. In Ottawa, on September 19, 2011, Canada became the first country to sign the *Ottawa Protocol to Combat anti-Semitism*.

> "The government of Canada took an historic step yesterday by signing the Ottawa Protocol to combat anti-Semitism. By doing so, it recognized anti-Semitism as a pernicious evil and a global threat against the Jewish people, the State of Israel and free, democratic countries everywhere. As Prime Minister Stephen Harper has noted, "Those who would hate and destroy the Jewish people would ultimately hate and destroy the rest of us as well."

The protocol is a declaration that hatred of this nature will not be tolerated in this country. It sets out an action plan for supporting initiatives that combat anti-Semitism and provides a framework for other nations to follow.

In announcing the Protocols, the then Foreign Affairs Minister John Baird expressed his government's **unequivocal support for the**

State of Israel. When the Palestinians threatened to unilaterally declare a state, referring to the turmoil at the United Nations, Minister Baird said,

> *"Canada will not stand behind Israel at the United Nations, we will stand right beside it. It is never a bad thing to do the right thing."*

Every person of conscience should take note of the Ottawa Protocols and never forget the lessons of the Holocaust when the world was silent.

CANADA, A LEADER IN THE FIGHT AGAINST ANTI-SEMITISM & TERROR

On Tuesday, January 27th, 2015, the world recognized 70 years since the liberation of Auschwitz-Birkenau, the German Nazi Concentration and Extermination Camp, which coincided with the 10th annual International Day of Commemoration in Memory of the Victims of the Holocaust. This solemn occasion was marked with commemorations around the world and in Canada's capital.

The Hon. Tim Uppal, then Minister of State for Multiculturalism, represented the Government of Canada in Poland to pay tribute to the victims of the Holocaust and Nazi genocide. During his speech honouring the survivors, Minister Uppal stated:

> *"Canada is a leader in the international fight against anti-Semitism because it is a Canadian tradition to stand for what is principled and just. Our government is dedicated to ensuring future generations understand the lessons of the Holocaust in order to prevent acts of hate and genocide."*
>
> http://canadianimmigrant.ca/slider/canada-commemorates-70th-anniversary-of-the-liberation-of-auschwitz-birkenau

The Honorable Jason Kenney, then Minister of Defence and Minister for Multiculturalism said in his speech:

> *"We must continue to commemorate and honour the victims of this uniquely sadistic, brutal and rampant atrocity perpetrated*

by the Nazis already now seven decades ago. To put it simply we must always remember, and never forget, and heaven forbid never permit another Holocaust to occur. This is the kind of resolution we must make at every opportunity, as I myself did on behalf of Canadians in attending the 65th anniversary of the liberation of Auschwitz Birkenau in 2010 in Poland, and just as my colleague Minister of State Tim Uppal has done in representing Canada there earlier today."

http://news.gc.ca/web/article-en.do?nid=967559

STEPHEN HARPER'S MORAL LEADERSHIP

In an article in the Jerusalem Post, January 16, 2014, David Weinberg stated the following:

"It's hard to comprehend the depth and consistency of Canada's strong support for Israel in recent years without appreciating the deep moral underpinnings of Prime Minister Stephen J. Harper's worldview."

"Canada has proven once again that morals come before political expediency, and that policy must reflect principles and values," President Shimon Peres said when Canada cut diplomatic relations with Iran in 2012. "I thank Canada for taking a stance based on the highest morals, and hope that other nations will see Canada as a role model."

Four Pillars that Undergird Prime Minister Harper's Approach

First, the Holocaust weighs heavily on Harper's mind, and colors his view of world affairs. *"Remembering the Holocaust is not merely an act of historical recognition, but an undertaking. The same threats exist today... Memory requires a solemn responsibility to fight those threats... And unfortunately, Israel remains a country under threat – threatened by those groups and regimes who deny to this day its right to exist,"* Harper said in 2006.

Second, Harper clearly understands the nature and dangers of modern anti-Semitism. His government has explicitly adopted Natan Sharansky's 3-D rubric, and slammed the "constant barrage of rhetorical Demonization, Double standards, and Delegitimization of Israel." In fact, the government has signed and endorsed the Ottawa Protocol on Combating Anti-Semitism (developed at the 2010 meeting in Ottawa of the Inter-Parliamentary Coalition for Combating Anti-Semitism), which is the only global working definition and concrete plan for combating anti-Semitism, especially state-sanctioned anti-Semitism.

Harper: "Why does Israel remain under threat? Make no mistake; look beyond the thinly veiled rationalizations. They [Israel's enemies] hate Israel, just as they hate the Jewish people. Our government believes that **those who threaten Israel also threaten Canada**, because, as the last world war showed, hate-fueled bigotry against some is ultimately a threat to us all, and must be resisted wherever it may lurk."

Harper's similarly impressive foreign minister, John Baird, said: "Harnessing disparate anti-Semitic, anti-American and anti-Western ideologies, the 'New Anti-Semitism' targets the Jewish people by targeting the Jewish homeland, Israel, as the source of injustice and conflict in the world, and uses, perversely, the language of human rights to do so. We must be relentless in exposing this New Anti-Semitism for what it is."

Third, Harper's government clearly sees Israel as Canada's "friend and ally in the democratic family of nations."

Speaking to the Herzliya Conference in 2012, Baird said that "Israel embodies values that Canada holds dear and respects. Israel is a beacon of light in a region that craves freedom, democracy, human rights and the rule of law."

Fourth, Harper takes a meta-historic view of Israel's resurgence as a modern nation-state. Speaking on Israel's 60th anniversary, he mused poetically about Zionism. "From shattered Europe and other countries near and far, the descendants of Abraham, Isaac and Jacob made their way home. Their pilgrimage was the culmination of a 2,000-year-old dream; it is a tribute to the unquenchable human aspiration for freedom, and a testament to the indomitable spirit of the Jewish people."

"Soon," he said, "I hope to have the opportunity to travel to Israel to see the 'miracle' with my own eyes; to see how millions of people from all over the earth, with their countless different languages and traditions, came together to build a modern, prosperous, vibrant, democratic country. It is a pilgrimage I have wanted to make for a long time, but my determination to do so was redoubled this spring after I visited Auschwitz."

"I want to see first-hand what the survivors of the Holocaust and their descendants have accomplished, for theirs is truly an achievement of resilience and renewal unsurpassed in human history. **I also want to go to deliver in person the message of Canada's unshakable support for Israel.**"

Harper has gone even further, saying that "the persistence of the Jewish homeland is a sign of hope and a symbol of our faith in humanity's future, in the power of good over evil." There is a diplomatic price to be paid for such principled defense of Israel. Yet Harper is undeterred.

"The easy thing to do," he told the Ottawa conference on anti-Semitism, "is simply to just get along and go along with this anti-Israeli rhetoric, to pretend it is just being even-handed, and to excuse oneself with the label of 'honest broker.' **[But] Canada will take a stand [in support of Israel], whatever the cost.**"

- "Not just because it is the right thing to do, but because history shows us, and the ideology of the anti-Israeli mob tells us all too well, that those who threaten the existence of the Jewish people are, in the longer term, a threat to all of us."

- Prime Minister Harper has made good on his words. As detailed in these pages, the Harper governments since 2006 have *consistently backed Israel's defensive actions against terrorists, and stood up for Israel in the international community at the most critical moments.*

- *To recall just one example: At the important G8 summit in 2011, Prime Minister Harper single-handedly blocked an American draft that sought to specify Israel's pre-1967 borders as the starting point for peace talks, because the resolution ignored other key issues such as recognition of Israel as a Jewish state and demilitarization of a Palestinian state. Harper stood up to enormous pressure from US President Obama and then-French president Nicolas Sarkozy.*

- *In the end, G8 leaders conceded the merit of Stephen Harper's position, and issued a balanced statement urging Israel and the Palestinians to resume negotiations (with no mention of the 1967 lines).*

- *In acting in this way, Harper has emerged as a voice of critique, courage and principle in a world that is in danger of losing its conscience about Jews and Israel.*

- *Harper believes that in the long run moral stances are the most pragmatic positions of all. He believes that the pragmatic and often cynical calculations that characterize so much of modern diplomacy bring ruin to the global order.*

- *For Israelis, this is very important. I, and many of my friends, relatives and colleagues in this country, frequently feel very much isolated from today's global community, a world which appears to be increasingly indifferent to Israel's existential dilemmas.*

- *Alas, this is a world in which the leadership of Iran vows to erase Israel, asserts that the Holocaust never happened, and continues to build a nuclear weapon – while receiving applause at the UN in New York, and praise for "moderation" in Geneva and Washington.*

- *Prime Minister Harper's bold words and actions give Israelis hope that there are indeed many decent people, some of them in positions of power, who will not bow to demonization or to the Orwellian twisting of language and history that habitually pertains to Israel these days.*

"Thank you, Prime Minister Harper, for not despairing of the world or abandoning Israel and the Jewish People." David Weinberg

KING DAVID AWARD

On May 21, 2015 Prime Minister Harper received the King David Award in honour of his principled support of Israel and Jewish communities worldwide during the King David Award Gala, hosted by the Jewish Community Council of Montreal. The Award was bestowed upon him, also, for his clear and consistent defence of Israel and his moral stance against anti-Semitism.

The prime minister received thunderous applause from more than a thousand guests who attended in his honour, for Bill C-51, anti-terrorism legislation.

He also affirmed Israel's right to defend itself.

"Israel's leadership has no choice but, at all times, to take the force it needs to protect what its enemies wish to destroy," he said. *"The only difference between Hamas and Israel, and ISIS and us, is that Hamas is closer to Israel. Israel is on the front lines. Those who turn a blind eye to Israel's enemies do so in the long run at their own peril."* Harper also said: *"Our foreign policy is different from the approach in the past, when we were trying to be liked by every dictator with a vote at the United Nations...We refuse to be neutral."*

Harper was praised throughout the evening in the most effusive terms and received several standing ovations, accolades of praise along with shouts and whistles. *(See more at: http://www.cjnews.com/news/montreal-event-hails-harper-modern-king-david#sthash.uczrN6dg.dpuf)*

GOD KEEP YOUR LAND GLORIOUS AND FREE

To stand on guard for Canada is to stand on guard for Israel. The Biblical imperative to bless Israel brings the blessing and favor of God upon any individual or nation.

Genesis 12:3 *"Those who bless Israel, God will bless."*

Prime Minister Harper's support for Israel as a head of state was unprecedented. After almost 10 years in power, Stephen Harper and the Conservative Party were defeated in the federal election of 19 October 2015 by the Liberal Party under Justin Trudeau.

Following the Canadian election on Friday, October 23, 2015, Israeli Prime Minister Benjamin Netanyahu offered his congratulations to Prime Minister designate Justin Trudeau in a telephone call affirming the friendship of the two countries.

Regarding newly elected Prime Minister Justin Trudeau, Israel's ambassador to Canada, Rafael Barak said, *"Mr. Trudeau has been very consistent from the very beginning of his campaign, in expressing his support for Israel."*

http://torontostar.newspaperdirect.com/epaper/viewer.aspx

Canadians are praying that Prime Minister Justin Trudeau and his government will demonstrate both the moral conviction and courage to stand with Israel and continue the long standing bi-lateral relations and support of Israel.

New Canadian PM Trudeau Votes No on 16 Anti-Israel U.N. Resolutions

"GENEVA, Nov. 25, 2015 – UN Watch applauded Prime Minister Justin Trudeau's government for voting yesterday at the UN General Assembly to join the U.S. in opposing 6 resolutions singling out Israel, and for being on track to continue without change Canada's prior policy of firmly opposing repetitive, disproportionate and one-sided resolutions — all drafted by the Palestinians except for two by Syria —

that are designed to delegitimize Israel, the Middle East's only democracy. So far, with final plenary or initial committee votes on 19 of the 20 annual anti-Israel resolutions, Canada's voting record is entirely unchanged from last year. This upholds the UN Charter's principle of equal treatment of all nations, and prejudice to none."

(http://www.unwatch.org/new-canadian-pm-trudeau-votes-no-on-16-anti-israel-u-n-resolutions/)

Canada was one of eight nations of the 193 United Nations that opposed the resolutions. This is commendable. Canada continues to be a voice of moral clarity and courage at the United Nations.

On Monday, February 22, 2016, the House of Commons in Canada passed a motion condemning the anti-Israel Boycott, Divestment and Sanctions (BDS) movement. This is a commendable first step in recognizing the BDS movement for what it truly is ~ another brand of anti-Semitism. The DBS movement seeks only to delegitimize and demonize Israel. Prime Minister Justin Trudeau, as well as MPs Tony Clement and Michelle Rempel who brought this motion forward, and the 229 Members of Parliament who voted in support of the motion are to be applauded. The motion calls on the Canadian government to condemn any and all attempts by Canadian organizations, groups or individuals to promote the BDS movement both in Canada and abroad.

At a time when anti-Semitism is on the rise globally, it is a moral and Biblical imperative to stand with Israel and the Jewish people.

God keep Your land glorious and free.
O Israel, we stand on guard for thee.

Stirred by God's Noble Theme!

CHAPTER EIGHT

O CANADA, WE STAND ON GUARD FOR THEE

Revelation 2:7 *"He who has an ear, let him hear what the Spirit of God says..."*

The Apostle John, in the book of Revelation chapters two and three, wrote seven letters addressed to the seven leaders of the seven churches of Asia Minor. These describe what he had seen in a vision while on the Isle of Patmos.

Revelation 1:20 *"The mystery of the seven stars which you saw in My right hand, and the seven golden lampstands: The seven stars are the angels of the seven churches, and the seven lampstands which you saw are the seven churches."*

It is important to note the distinction that the letters were addressed to the *'angels'* of the churches. The word *'angels'* being interpreted, means *'messengers'* or *'key leaders'* or *'pastors.'* (Strong's 32 – Greek - angeloi) The letters were not addressed to the congregations in the churches but to those in authority.

Though specific and relevant to that time, the letters are timeless and have relevance even today. Of interest is the fact that each of the seven letters had seven components:

1) Greetings addressed to the leaders of a church
2) Descriptive title and characteristics of Jesus
3) Commendations
4) Criticisms
5) Instructions, warnings and a call to repent
6) Concluding exhortations
7) Rewards and promises for the overcomers

Three of the letters displayed a Biblical approach to addressing issues and matters of great concern. Commendations preceded correction. Three churches in particular were commended for their good deeds, hard work, enduring strength, steadfast faith, boldness in proclaiming the gospel and perseverance in tribulation. All deeds were observed, recorded and acknowledged. Heaven's gaze observed every detail and missed nothing! Heaven chronicled every act of kindness, their labours of love and their dedication. Though destitute in material goods yet strong in faith and rich in spirit, they were faithful and had not grown weary in well doing. They were exhorted to be resolute, steadfast and faithful unto the end.

The letters to the churches in Ephesus, Pergamum and Thyatira shared a common component. The commendations were followed by the words, *"Nevertheless I have this against you."* A statement such as this ought to arrest any recipient! As faithful and steadfast as these leaders in the churches were, there were serious concerns that needed to be addressed and amended. In all cases it was imperative that they repent or there would be consequences.

The word *'repent'* used in all instances in the New Testament is the word *'metanoeo'* (Strong's 3340) which means to think differently about a matter and to reconsider one's actions or position or to return to the beginning, to what was stated in the first place. In Hebrew thought, the word repent is *'shuwb'* (Strong's 7725) which means to turn back and go in the other direction. It also means to change your mind about a matter. The leaders of the churches who repented and changed their ways were promised great reward.

This Kingdom principle is clear. It is entirely possible for an individual, a church, an organization, a government or a nation to abound in noble achievements, great works, amazing endeavors, and exceptional accomplishments meriting outstanding accolades and honor, as with Ephesus, Pergamum and Thyatira, yet miss the mark in a very crucial and critical matter. This is sobering!

Governments and nations create constitutions, laws, charters and foreign policies. They have etched their ideologies in the scrolls of time. Some noble! Some ignoble! Many nations, such as Canada, have set their foundations, constitutions and policies on Godly Judeo-Christian Biblical principles. Others have fixed their cornerstones on ideologies that are tyrannical, dictatorial and/or oppressive.

From Heaven's perspective, the government of God is the model for mankind! The constitution of God found in the Bible ought to be the model for the nations of the world.

> **Isaiah 9:7** *"Of His government and of His peace there shall be no end!"*

> **Psalm 72:8** *"He shall have dominion from sea to sea from the river to the ends of the earth."*

It will be God's government and the laws of His Kingdom by which the nations of the world will be weighed in the balance and judged. God has clearly stated His noble constitution, His *Noble Theme*, in the Bible.

Nations of the world have crafted their foreign policies regarding the nation of Israel. God too has inscribed His foreign policy regarding His covenant land and His covenant people. His constitution stands firm forever. There is a very specific Kingdom dictate that emphatically exceeds and supersedes all man-made constitutions. God's foreign policy regarding Israel and the nations is rooted in the Abrahamic covenant inscribed in the eternal Word of God. Regarding His covenant land, God clearly and plainly declares it is His land. It is not to be sold or divided or carved up by Israel or the nations of the world. Did He not say, *"It is My Land ~ Do not divide?"*

It has been stated in previous chapters that the Word of God is enduring and stands firm forever. His Word stands true whether nations or individuals believe it and/or live by it or not. The Word of God applies to the nation of Israel and all nations of the world regardless of creed or religion.

In the book of Daniel, the heathen Babylonian King Belshazzar was weighed in the balance and found wanting. The story is sobering. Any individual, be it king or commoner, cannot do as he/she pleases and think that the universal laws of God, His Kingdom principles, warnings and judgements, spoken by the prophets, will not affect him or her.

King Belshazzar was banqueting with thousands of his lords and princes and wives and concubines. They were drinking from the golden vessels that were seized and stolen from the Temple of the Lord in Jerusalem and brought to Babylon. While drinking, the handwriting of God appeared on the wall. It was a strange writing that no one understood. Eventually Daniel, in whom was the Spirit of wisdom, understanding and interpretation, was summoned to decipher the words. God's judgement fell on King Belshazzar for his heart was not humbled. He lifted himself against the Lord and did not glorify the God of Israel. He was weighed in the balance and found wanting in one very critical matter. *"Nevertheless I have this against you."* One crucial matter tipped the scales and the king lost his kingdom. His empire was ripped from His hands and given to the Medes and Persians. Is there a lesson to be learned? Is there a warning to be heeded? Is there a pitfall to avoid? Is there wisdom to be gleaned?

Simply stated, it is imperative at any given time in history for kings, leaders and people in general to know the Word of God and find out what God has to say about certain matters that He deems holy, precious and sacred. Whether a king or nation acknowledges God's Word or not, it forever remains in effect. God's universal laws, as with the laws of nature, like sowing and reaping or the laws of gravity, remain perpetually effective. God's moral, judicial, civil and ceremonial laws all bear consequences when not observed or heeded. God is Sovereign!

CANADA AND THE TWO-STATE SOLUTION

God's covenant land is not to be divided! *"He who has an ear, let him hear what the Spirit of God is saying..."*

Canada's cup of praise overflows with respect to our government's unprecedented support, friendship and solidarity with Israel, as clearly highlighted in the previous chapter. With a deep sense of gratitude and national pride we commend our Canadian government.

In light of Canada's unwavering support for Israel, there is however one matter of grave concern. A matter worthy of sombre consideration. In like manner, the words spoken to the leaders in the churches in Ephesus, Pergamum and Thyatira from the book of Revelation, hang in the air... *"Nevertheless I have this against you."*

Some of the statements in *Canada's Policy on Key Issues in the Israeli-Palestinian Conflict* stand in glaring violation and contradiction to the Word of God. Canada's official position clearly supports a 'two-state solution'. Canada has joined the peace talks and 'land for peace' proposals in an effort either to support and/or pressure Israel to divide her covenant land with intent to create a Palestinian state. Press releases are posted on the Canadian Ministry of Foreign Affairs website stating details of the policy, monetary contributions allocated to the Palestinians and progress on the implementation of the policy.

The Ministry of Foreign Affairs, Trade and Development Canada, has published on its website, an official policy entitled: *Canadian Policy on Key Issues in the Israeli-Palestinian Conflict.* It can be viewed in its entirety on the official government website of Foreign Affairs, Trade and Development Canada:

http://www.international.gc.ca/name-anmo/peace_process-processus_paix/canadian_policy-politique_canadienne.aspx?lang=eng

Some of the articles in the Foreign Policy are commendable and a source of national pride:

> *"Canada supports Israel's right to live in peace with its neighbours within secure boundaries and recognizes Israel's right to assure its own security. Israel has a right under international law to take the necessary measures, in accordance with human rights and international humanitarian law, to protect the security of its citizens from attacks by terrorist groups. Canada and Israel enjoy a steadfast friendship and strong, growing bilateral relations in many areas based on shared values, including democracy."*

Considering all that has been stated in this book regarding the consequences of dividing God's covenant land, Israel, it is a profoundly grave concern that Canada's foreign policy supports a 'two-state solution'.

> *"Canada recognizes the Palestinian right to self-determination and supports the creation of **a sovereign, independent, viable, democratic and territorially contiguous Palestinian state**, as part of a comprehensive, just and lasting peace settlement. **Canada also strongly supports the Quartet's Road Map**, which sets out the obligations of both parties and steps for **establishment of a Palestinian state**. Canada supports resolutions that are consistent with Canadian policy on the Middle East that are rooted in international law, reflect current dynamics and contribute to the goal of a **negotiated 'two-state solution'** to the Arab-Israeli conflict."*

Prime Minister Stephen Harper publically stated support for a 'two-state solution'. On Saturday, January 18, 2014, before Prime Minister Harper's first trip to Israel, his spokesman, Jason MacDonald, as reported in the Ottawa Citizen Newspaper, stated:

> *"I speak on behalf of the Prime Minister, 'the goal is a negotiated agreement that results in the **two states**....an Israel in which people can live in peace and security, and a viable, independent and secure Palestinian state. **We would like to see a 'two-state solution'.**'"*

On Sunday, March 22, 2015, Prime Minister Stephen Harper reiterated Canada's support for a 'two-state solution' for Israelis and Palestinians during a phone call to newly re-elected Israeli Prime Minister Benjamin Netanyahu.

(http://www.cbc.ca/news/canada/canada-supports-two-state-solution-stephen-harper-tells-benjamin-netanyahu-1.3004891)

Articles posted in the Canadian National Post Newspaper, the Jerusalem Post and other media outlets, address Canada's discrepancy between the Federal Conservative government's public support for Israel and official policy statements on the Canadian Ministry of Foreign Affairs website:

> *"Prime Minster Harper and Canada's official policy on Israel: Are they compatible?" (Jerusalem Post, Tuesday, January 14, 2014)*

> *"Harper government's strong Israel stance not matched by official Foreign Affairs Policies, former Israeli Ambassador Alan Baker says." (National Post, January 14, 2014)*

The following was printed in the National Post Canadian newspaper on Jan. 14, 2014:

> *"McGill University professor Rex Brynan, who has been intimately following the Israeli-Palestinian conflict for years, suggested this ambiguity is a deliberate aspect of the government's approach to the Middle East. "It's not inconvenient to have variations in policy that you can point people to," he said, "because when the government gets criticized on the Arab side, they can say, "Well, look at the website." (National Post, January 14, 2014)*

ISRAEL AND THE TWO-STATE SOLUTION

Two political parties in the Israeli Knesset (government), Yahad and Bayit Yehudi, believe God promised the land of Israel. They believe the eternal bond between the Jewish people and their land is not subject to negotiation. They call for the annexation of all of Judea and Samaria to the State of Israel and promise to strengthen the settlement enterprise in all of the West Bank.

Other parties in the Knesset believe in a 'two-state solution' with varying positions regarding the status of Jerusalem and the settlements in the West Bank.

An article posted in the Jerusalem Post just before the March 2015 Israeli federal election stated the position of several of the major political parties on the Israeli-Palestinian Peace Process.

(http://www.jpost.com/Arab-Israeli-Conflict/How-the-parties-stand-on-the-Israeli-Palestinian-peace-process-394028)

On Wednesday, May 20th, 2015, in an article posted in the Jerusalem Post, Prime Minister Benjamin Netanyahu publicly pledged his support for 'two-state solution' to the Israeli-Palestinian conflict, in his first clear policy statement on the issue since his new government was formed earlier in May.

(http://www.jpost.com/Arab-Israeli-Conflict/Netanyahu-to-EU-foreign-ministerI-support-the-vision-of-two-states-for-two-people-403685)

DO NOT DIVIDE MY LAND

The Bible is replete with occurrences where men and women of God delivered the Word of the Lord with power, conviction and authority. Divinely inspired Words came as instruction, direction, edification, rebuke and warning. Stirred by the Spirit of God, His Word was conveyed by His prophets to individuals, nations and kings. God continues to speak through men and women today. Such is the case of a man of God, Dr. Robert Mawire, a minister from Africa who was pastoring a church in Texas.

In 1998, Robert Mawire stood before Prime Minister Benjamin Netanyahu and told him that the day he would negotiate 'land for peace', his government would fall. Robert went on to say that the time for Israel to turn to God had come. It was time to stand on the Word of God. His Word is Truth. Robert said, to Prime Minister Netanyahu, *"You shall not divide 'My' land or negotiate 'My' 'land for peace' or your government will collapse."*

Mr. Netanyahu laughed quietly and dismissed him. In October, 1998 Prime Minister Netanyahu negotiated the Wye River land-for-peace deal in the West Bank with Yasser Arafat. Several months later, Netanyahu's government collapsed and he was out of office.

On April 16, 2001, Netanyahu met Robert Mawire again along with Ron Nachman, mayor of Ariel, a settlement in Israel, at a church in Florida where Mr. Netanyahu would speak. Dr. Mawire stepped forward and handed Netanyahu a plaque with these inscriptions:

"The God of Abraham, Isaac, and Jacob has chosen you to be the 'father' of His people and to restore the Tabernacle of David. You will once again become Prime Minister of Israel, and God has appointed Ron Nachman to be your right hand man, as it was with Joshua and Moses.

If you honor His covenant that He made with Abraham, Isaac, and Jacob regarding Israel, He will honor you and exalt you. But if you disregard His covenant and give away His land, He will dishonor you.

Joshua 1: 6-7,9 *"Be strong and of good courage: for unto this people shalt thou divide for an inheritance the land, which I sware unto their fathers to give them. Only be thou strong and very courageous, that thou mayest observe to do according to all the law, which Moses my servant commanded thee: turn not from it to the right hand or to the left, that thou mayest prosper whithersoever thou goest. Have I not commanded thee? Be strong and of good courage; be not afraid, neither be thou dismayed: for the LORD thy God is with thee whithersoever thou goest."* (KJV)

From the Servant of God, Robert Mawire, Fort Worth, Texas, 2001

Mawire then spoke to Netanyahu: *"God is not done with you. You will be prime minister again at a critical time in history. Don't ever negotiate* 'land for peace' *again."* In 2009, Netanyahu became Israeli prime minister once more.

Dr. Mawire met with Mr. Netanyahu many times and together they examined the Word of God, the prophecies and promises regarding the restoration of the land of Israel. God opened Benjamin Netanyahu's heart to believe that Israel's existence today is a miracle and God is at work fulfilling Bible prophecy.

Read more about this extraordinary story from the Times of Israel, March 17, 2015: *http://blogs.timesofisrael.com/netanyahu-and-an-undivided-jerusalem/* This story is also recounted by Ron Nachman and Robert Mawire's mutual friend, Ray Bentley, in his 2014 book The Holy Land Key.

In addition, Robert Mawire met Ariel Sharon in 2001 and delivered the Word of the Lord to him. He said, *"You will be prime minister in six months and you are going to be used by the Lord to protect the children of Israel. God wants you to never, never negotiate* 'land for peace' *because God owns the land. God wants you to stand on His promises and you will be secure and your government will be stronger. However, the day you disobey the Lord, He will strike you."*

True to the Word of the Lord, Ariel Sharon became Israel's next Prime Minister in six months. In 2005 however, Ariel Sharon orchestrated Israel's unilateral disengagement from the Gaza strip. He suffered a stroke on January 4, 2006 and remained in a permanent vegetative state until his death in January 2014.

The God of Abraham, Isaac and Jacob speaks today. Thus saith the Lord,

> **Joel 3:2,3** *"I will also gather all nations, And bring them down to the Valley of Jehoshaphat; And I will enter into judgment with them there On account of My people, My heritage Israel, Whom they have scattered among the nations; They have also divided up My land. They have cast lots for My people,…"*

God is settling His People back in the land of Israel never to be uprooted again. He is restoring the ancient ruins and rebuilding the ancient cities. He is restoring the land to the people and the people to the land.

Kings and people of Israel, kings and people of nations, *"Heed the Word of the Lord. Do not divide My land! Do not negotiate My 'land for peace'! Do not give away My 'land for peace'!"*

CONNECTING THE DOTS
COINCIDENCE OR CONSEQUENCE

The Bible is clear. Our loving and just God has warned both Israel and the nations that there would be consequences for those seeking to divide His covenant land, the promised-land given to the Jewish people. Joel's warning cannot be ignored.

> **Joel 3:2,3** *"... I will enter into judgment with them there on account of **My people, My heritage** Israel, whom they have scattered among the nations; They have also divided up **My land**. They have cast lots for My people."*

> *Supporting Greater Prosperity and Security for Palestinians:* "Headlines of a News Release posted on Foreign Affairs, Trade and Development, Canada website. **June 17, 2013:** *Foreign Affairs Minister John Baird today visited the West Bank to announce an immediate, $25-million contribution to aid Palestinians. Baird announced up to $1.4 million in new support to the Office of the Quartet Representative. (see Quartet below) An additional $3.6 million will further the Palestinian Authority's security system reforms and strengthen the rule of law in the West Bank. The Honourable Julian Fantino, Minister of International Cooperation, said from Ottawa that an additional $20 million in development assistance builds on previous Canadian contributions of $300 million over five years and will help meet urgent food and health needs while Canada considers future funding."*

(http://www.international.gc.ca/media/aff/news-communiques/2013/06/17a.aspx?lang=eng)

> "Working with its partners and through the United Nations, its agencies and other organizations, Canada continues to support and respond to the humanitarian and development needs of the Palestinian people. At the Paris Donors Conference in December 2007, Canada announced a commitment of $300 million over 5 years towards improving Palestinian security, governance and prosperity."

(http://www.international.gc.ca/name-anmo/peace_process-processus_paix/canadian_policy-politique_canadienne.aspx?lang=eng#a01)

Assistance from the international community for humanitarian aid and security to any nation is commendable provided there is an accountability that allocated funds are used for stated purposes and not apportioned toward terrorism, incitement or indoctrination to destroy any other people group. Accountability and follow-up measures are imperative for obvious reasons.

Quartet Road Map for Peace: *The roadmap for peace was a plan to resolve the Israeli–Palestinian conflict proposed by the Quartet on the Middle East: the United States, the European Union, Russia and the United Nations. The principles of the plan, originally drafted by U.S. Foreign Service Officer Donald Blome, were first outlined by U.S. President George W. Bush in a speech on June 24th, 2002 in which he called for an independent Palestinian state living side by side with Israel, in peace.* (http://en.wikipedia.org/wiki/Road_map_for_peace)

Nowhere in searching out the Canadian Government websites, could I find a press release about a Canadian minister having travelled to Israel to promote the peace process and the 'two-state solution', prior to Minister Baird's visit to Ramallah and Jerusalem. Immediately following Minister Baird's visit in April, 2013, consequences ensued.

JUST ASKING

Could it be coincidence or consequence that immediately following former Minister of Foreign Affairs John Baird's visit to Ramallah on **June 17th, 2013**, meeting with the Palestinians, and then in Jerusalem, meeting with the Israelis, and his meeting with Tony Blair leading the Quartet, that a catastrophic disaster occurred on Canadian soil in the city of Calgary? One might reasonably ask, *"Why Calgary?"*

Could it be coincidence or consequence that the catastrophic disaster occurred in Prime Minister Harper's home riding of Calgary?

> *"In the days leading up to **June 19, 2013**, Alberta, Canada, experienced heavy rainfall that triggered **catastrophic flooding described by the provincial government as the worst in Alberta's history**. Areas along the Bow, Elbow, Highwood, Red Deer, Sheep, Little Bow, and South Saskatchewan rivers and their tributaries were particularly affected. A total of 32 states of local emergency were declared and 28 emergency operations centers were activated as water levels rose and numerous communities were placed under evacuation orders. **Five people were confirmed dead** as a direct result of the flooding and over **100,000 people were displaced throughout the region**. Some 2,200 Canadian Forces (CF) troops were deployed to help in flooded areas. **Total damage estimates exceeded C$5 billion** and in terms of insurable damages, is the **costliest disaster in Canadian history** at $1.7 billion. Receding waters gave way to a mammoth cleanup of affected areas."*

(http://en.wikipedia.org/wiki/2013_Alberta_floods)

The catastrophic flood was reported by the television news outlets as a bizarre and freak occurrence. It was reported on national TV that the weather systems normally move from the Rocky Mountains in the west, on to the foothills over the Calgary region and then typically move eastward eventually dissipating over the Prairie Provinces. However, this particular weather system strangely hovered over Calgary for two days and dropped record levels of rain, resulting in unprecedented flooding. It was unexplainable and perplexing as reported by the media and weather experts.

According to data tracked by Alberta's Ministry of Environment and Sustainable Resource Development,

> *"In the space of a day or two, the flows of the three rivers rocketed up five to ten times their normal rates."*
> (http://en.wikipedia.org/wiki/2013_Alberta_floods)

Could there be a connection with Canada's foreign policy on the 'two-state solution' and the succession of catastrophies dubbed by the media as *'freak'* events that occurred in Calgary, Alberta, Prime Minister Harper's riding?

- **A freak snow storm hit Calgary in early October**, still considered to be summer. Headlines read: Cost of cleaning up Calgary's freak snowstorm-damaged trees expected to hit $18M. *(http://www.calgarysun.com/2014/10/06/cost-of-cleaning-up-calgarys-freak-snowstorm-damaged-trees-expected-to-hit-18m)*

- **More than half of severe weather insurance claims in 2013 in Canada came from Alberta.** Albertans took the brunt of severe weather damage last year as evidenced by more than half of insurance losses being claimed by victims of natural catastrophes. May 10, 2013. *(http://www.calgarysun.com/2013/05/10/more-than-half-of-severe-weather-insurance-claims-in-canada-came-from-alberta)*

- **Underground fire in Calgary's downtown will cut power to thousands of homes for up to a week:** October 12, 2014 *(http://www.calgarysun.com/2014/10/12/underground-fire-in-calgarys-downtown-will-cut-power-to-thousands-of-homes-for-up-to-a-week)*

- **Calgary's downtown staying dark until Thursday, city sets up lodging centre for displaced residents.** The city has set up an emergency shelter with rising demand from displaced residents for temporary lodging nearing capacity. October 13, 2014 *(http://www.calgarysun.com/2014/10/13/enmax-officials-hope-to-return-power-to-calgarys-downtown-by-mid-week-following-electrical-fire)*

- Damage to downtown Calgary's electrical system from a fire Saturday will require a rebuild, not just repairs. Under-ground electrical fire caused a power outage in a large part of the downtown core affecting approximately 2,100 businesses and 5,000 residents. October 13, 2014 *(http://www.cbc.ca/news/canada/calgary/downtown-calgary-electrical-fire-damage-will-take-days-to-fix-require-rebuild-1.2796497)*

- Calgary police lay charges in pro Palestinian rally assaults. In a rare and unprecedented demonstration, hundreds of pro-Palestinian supporters had converged outside city hall, July 18, 2014. *(http://www.calgarysun.com/2014/08/12/calgary-police-lay-charges-in-pro-palestinian-rally-assaults)*

- Hail storms that pummeled Airdrie, (a city within the Calgary region,) deemed catastrophic, will likely hike insurance rates. The cost of storms Aug. 7 and 8 that hit Airdrie with golf ball-sized or larger hail stones are over $25 million. August 12, 2014 *(http://www.calgarysun.com/2014/08/12/hails-storms-that-pummeled-airdrie-deemed-catastrophic-will-likely-hike-insurance-rates)*

- Five students murdered in Brentwood, NW Calgary, Alta. On Thursday April 17, 2014. Chaplains called in to comfort in the aftermath of mass murder. *(http://www.calgarysun.com/2014/04/17/helping-cops-cope-with-catastrophe—chaplains-called-in-to-comfort-in-aftermath-of-mass-murder)*

CONSERVATIVE SCANDALS MULTIPLYING BY THE DAY

In April 2013, after Baird's visit to Ramallah and Israel, a litany of scandals and mismanagement allegations in the Conservative government suddenly came to the fore. From Mike Duffy, Nigel Wright, Pamela Wallen to robocalls and patronage-tainted hirings, they were unlike anything the Conservatives encountered in the previous seven years of the Harper government.

(http://o.canada.com/news/national/conservative-scandals-multiplying-by-the-day)

Could it be coincidence or consequence that all these scandals broke out at the same time Canadian Cabinet Ministers were in Ramallah and Jerusalem affirming Canada's position on the 'two-state policy?'

Ironically, it is of interest to note that the Canadian Conservative Party Convention was scheduled to take place on June 27, 2013 in Calgary but was cancelled due to the catastrophic floods.

The talk of the town and the 'buzz' on the Hill reflected the decline in the polls and was punctuated in Canadian newspapers. Some headlines and comments stated:

- Conservatives prepare to gather after scandalous spring. *(Ottawa Citizen, June 22, 2013)*

- It's up to the party base to rescue the Conservatives *(Ottawa Citizen, June 22, 2013)*

- Stephen Harper looks to woo Tories: Upcoming speech at Conservative convention and reported cabinet shuffle seen as efforts to regain control of political agenda. Stephen Harper will use a speech to Conservative Party faithful next week to try to rebuild relations with rank-and-file Tories disenchantment by the senate expense scandals. *(Ottawa Citizen, Saturday, June 22, 2013)*

- Prime Minister Harper is reported to be rebooting his cabinet by late or early August in hopes to re-energize his party. *(Ottawa Citizen, Saturday, June 22, 2013)*

- How can Harper hold on? It would have been hard to imagine a few months ago, but Conservatives are now openly bemoaning what Canada might be like under Prime Minister Thomas Mulcair or Prime Minister Justin Trudeau. *(Ottawa Citizen, Saturday, June 22, 2013)*

- For the first time, the true believers are losing faith: The more than 3,000 delegates at the federal Conservative convention in Calgary next week will likely be talking about something that, at past conventions, Conservatives didn't have to wrestle with – scandal! *(Ottawa Citizen, Saturday, June 22, 2013)*

• MPs expect they'll be commiserating with constituents and trying to figure out if the Tory brand has been irreparably damaged. *(Ottawa Citizen, Saturday, June 22, 2013)*

CONSERVATIVES DECLINE IN THE POLLS

In April 2013, the then Minister of Foreign Affairs John Baird visited Ramallah, West Bank, pledging millions of Canadian dollars to build an independent Palestinian state.

***Baird Consults in the West bank. April 6, 2013** - Foreign Affairs Minister John Baird today made the following statement: "Canada committed **$300 million** over five years with a focus on assisting security and development in the West Bank. Some of the projects are still underway, and I assured Palestinian leaders that we will see our existing commitments through. Canada remains committed to a '**two-state solution**' to the Israel-Palestinian matter, one reached through a negotiated agreement that guarantees Israel's right to live in peace and security and leads to the establishment of a Palestinian state. (http://www.international.gc.ca/media/aff/news-communiques/2013/04/06a.aspx?lang=eng)*

Could it be coincidence or consequence that during Minister Baird's visit to Israel in April 2013, the Canadian polling tables turned in favor of the Liberal party? A very dramatic shift in the political landscape transpired. The leadership race for the Liberal Party took place at that time. In Ottawa, the party announced Justin Trudeau as its new leader on April 14, 2013.

Could it be coincidence or consequence that when Canada engaged in more active participation in the Israeli-Palestinian peace plans that the majority Conservative government dropped in the Canadian polls? As Canada's participation in the peace process continued, the Liberals held their lead in the Canadian polls.

The following table provides a compilation of scientific, nation-wide public opinion polls that have been conducted since the 2011 Canadian federal election and leading up to the 42nd Canadian federal election to take place in 2015. The crossover date of the downturn of the Conservative party was April 2013, the precise date that Minister Baird visited Ramallah and Jerusalem to promote Canada's position regarding the 'two-state solution'.

(http://en.wikipedia.org/wiki/Opinion_polling_for_the_42nd_Canadian_federal_election)

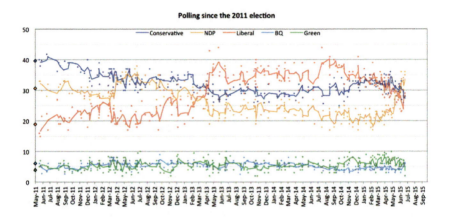

Throughout the federal election campaign of 2015, the ConservativeParty when issuing statements condemning terror attacks in Israel, also included statements advocating Canada's position supporting the 'two-state solution'.

Statement by the Minister of Foreign Affairs Hon. Rob Nicholson condemning attacks in Jerusalem ~ October 4, 2015

The Hon. Rob Nicholson, P.C., Q.C. and Conservative Party candidate for Niagara Falls, today issued the following statement:

"Canada condemns in the strongest of terms recent stabbing attacks in the Old City of Jerusalem that left two Israelis dead and others injured, including a baby. Our thoughts and prayers are with the family and friends of the victims as well as those of the Israeli couple shot dead in front of their children just days ago.

"The timing of these attacks is especially deplorable as Jews around the world prepare to celebrate the Jewish holiday of Simchat Torah.

"The escalation of violence that we have witnessed over the past few days will do nothing to advance the interests of peace.

"As we have said before, Canada will always stand with Israel. Our position is that Israel's right to exist is absolute and non-negotiable, and we will oppose efforts to undermine Israel's legitimacy or right to defend herself in the face of terror.

"A re-elected Conservative government will continue to advocate a negotiated 'two-state solution' that will enable Israelis and Palestinians to live in security."

Statement by the Hon. Jason Kenney condemning attacks across Israel ~ October 14, 2015

The Hon. Jason Kenney today issued the following statement:

"Canada condemns in the strongest terms possible the recent wave of terror attacks against Israeli civilians that has resulted in a number of tragic deaths and injuries. Our thoughts and prayers are with the families and friends of the victims.

"We are deeply concerned by escalating incitement and violence that does nothing to advance the interests of peace, stability, and security in the region. There can be no justification for these attacks, and we will continue to oppose efforts undermine Israel's legitimacy or right to defend herself in the face of terror.

"As we have stated, a re-elected Conservative government will continue to advocate a negotiated 'two-state solution' that will enable Israelis and Palestinians to live in security."

Could it be coincidence or a consequence of the Conservative 'two-state policy' that the results of the federal election on Monday, October 19th, 2015 saw Stephen Harper's government succumb to a sweeping victory for Justin Trudeau and the Liberal party? If God's Word says that He will enter into judgement against the nation who seeks to divide His land, could this be one of those judgements? Just asking!

> *"The 11-week campaign for Canada's 42nd general election was the longest and costliest in Canadian history. It involved a fair share of ups and downs for each party involved. At one point, it was a three-way race. There was a time when the NDP surged ahead. The Conservatives looked like they would form another minority government for a long time. But in the end – as the public mood shifted over the final week or two as it often does – Liberal Leader Justin Trudeau won a majority government."*

http://www.theglobeandmail.com/news/politics/how-the-trudeau-liberals-won-a-majority-in-the-2015-federalelection/article27048562/T

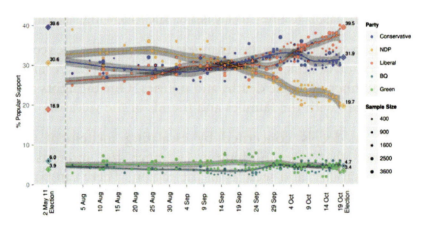

Canada and some of the international community do not recognize permanent Israeli control over territories *'occupied'* in 1967 (the Golan Heights, the West Bank, East Jerusalem and the Gaza Strip) and deems Israel as an *'occupying power.'* This is the wording used in Canada's Foreign Policy.

(http://www.international.gc.ca/name-anmo/peace_process-processus_paix/canadian_policy-politique_canadienne.aspx?lang=eng)

Keeping in mind the same Biblical principle and patterns outlined in previous chapters, and **Obadiah 15** *"As you have done (to Israel), it shall be done to you,"* the Golden Lake Algonquin land claim has been set at no less than 117,500 acres. The land claim has come to the fore in recent years with Algonquin First Nation accusing the Canadian government of **'illegally occupying'** their native land!

An article published in the *Hill Times* Newspaper stated the following:

> *"Most Canadians are unaware that Parliament Hill sits on unceded Algonquin land. The House of Commons, the Senate, and the Supreme Court of Canada make laws for all Canadians while situated on land that was never lawfully purchased from the aboriginal owners, contrary to formal legal rules established in 1763."*
>
> (http://www.hilltimes.com/opinion-piece/2013/07/01/algonquin-land-claim-a-journey-of-reconciliation/35205)

Negotiations with federal and provincial governments and the Algonquin land claim have been ongoing for many years and still have a long way to go. The Algonquin never signed a treaty with the government of Canada nor its predecessors. Five of their communities are laying claim to a huge piece of land stretching from North Bay along the Mattawa and Ottawa Rivers. This includes Ottawa down to just short of Hawksbury on one side. On the other side the land claim does include Algonquin Park, Bancroft, Westport, north of Prescott, north of St. Andrews and back up the Ottawa River approaching Hawksbury. This is a vast area of about 250km by 100km.

Canada's First Nation's land claim is a very important and sensitive subject/issue in our nation. It is interesting to follow in light of a possible connection with Canada's Foreign Policy.

Could it be that there is a link between Canada's Foreign Policy stating Israel as an *'illegal occupying power'* on her God given covenant land and the First Nations land claim stating Canada as an *'illegal occupying power?'* Just asking!

Obadiah 15 *"As you have done (to Israel), it shall be done to you,"*

O CANADA, WE STAND ON GUARD FOR THEE

What does it mean to stand on guard for Canada? By definition, a sentinel who stands guard is a watchman who protects a sovereign's kingdom, property and people. If 99% of the affairs of a nation are in order but 1% opposes the Word of God, consequences will follow. If the 1% clearly stands in opposition to the Word of God over such a critical matter as some of the statements in Canada's foreign policy, then it becomes the weak link in the chain, the crack in the foundation or the opening in the gates that may cause calamitous consequences. Is there is a root issue or are there statements in a foreign policy that could invoke the judgements of God? It is a sobering consideration. If so, it must be identified, considered and changed.

The watchman must sound the alarm when danger is imminent and must not hold back. After having stated throughout this book the Biblical references and warnings about dividing God's Covenant land it is imperative to carefully and prayerfully reconsider portions of Canada's position and foreign policy with Israel, lest we find ourselves increasingly connecting the dots in a deluge of successive consequences.

A few questions must be tabled.

1) If a nation's foreign policy regarding Israel aligns with the Bible, will this bring increased blessing, security, favor and prosperity to that nation?

2) Conversely, if a nation's foreign policy regarding Israel contradicts the Bible, will this diminish or remove God's hand of blessing, protection, favor and prosperity proportionately? Will calamities ensue?

3) Does God's Word, *"As you do to Israel it shall be done to you,"* still bear weight today?

4) Does public support verbalized for Israel by a head of state carry more weight than a foreign policy that contradicts the Word of God posted on it's government website?

5) Does a nation's foreign policy that contradicts the Word of God posted on its government website carry more weight than public support verbalized for Israel made by a head of state?

6) Can a government's foreign policy affect the outcome of a federal election?

Blow the Trumpet in Zion

Isaiah 18:3 *"All inhabitants of the world and dwellers on the earth: When he lifts up a banner on the mountains, you see it; And when he blows a trumpet, you hear it."*

1 Corinthians 14:7 *"Even things without life, whether flute or harp, when they make a sound, unless they make a distinction in the sounds, how will it be known what is piped or played?"*

The distinctive sound of the trumpet blasts in Israel's history either indicated imminent danger, an approaching enemy, a call to battle, a time to break up camp or celebratory blasts signalling the feasts of the Lord.

The trumpet of God is resounding today in all the earth for the nations of the world, for governments, churches, organizations and individuals to come into alignment with the Word of God with respect to His covenant land. The sound of the alarm, the blast of the shofar is released today to those who are engaged in or support the 'two-state solution'. It is a reality that cannot be ignored. The sound is one of warning. Unless heeded, there will be consequences.

God is sounding His shofar from the pages of the Bible through the mouths of His prophets. Nations, hear the sound and come into alignment.

As for heads of state, global leaders and kings in the earth today, God clearly reveals in the Bible that He is the One who sets up and deposes kings.

Daniel 2:20,21 *"Blessed be the name of God forever and ever, For wisdom and might are His and He changes the times and the seasons;* ***He removes kings and raises up kings.****"*

With God, all things are possible. God has, as in time past, worked through heathen kings to carry out His divine purposes. King Cyrus of Persia (ancient Iran) is one example. God stirred Cyrus' heart to make a decree in accordance to a prophecy released through the Hebrew prophet Jeremiah, 70 years prior.

Ezra 1:1-4 *"Now in the first year of Cyrus king of Persia, that the word of the LORD by the mouth of Jeremiah might be fulfilled,* ***the LORD stirred up the spirit of Cyrus king of Persia, so that he made a proclamation throughout all his kingdom,*** *and also put it in writing, saying, 'Thus says Cyrus king of Persia: All the kingdoms of the earth the LORD God of heaven has given me. And He has commanded me to build Him a house at Jerusalem which is in Judah. Who is among you of all His people? May his God be with him, and let him go up to Jerusalem which is in Judah, and build the house of the LORD God of Israel (He is God), which is in Jerusalem. And whoever is left in any place where he dwells, let the men of his place help him with silver and gold, with goods and livestock, besides the freewill offerings for the house of God which is in Jerusalem."*

When God stirred Cyrus' heart to accomplish His will, He called Cyrus His shepherd, His anointed. He even bestowed upon him a title of honor because he did the Lord's bidding.

Isaiah 44:28 *"Who says of Cyrus, '****He is My shepherd, and he shall perform all My pleasure.****" Saying to Jerusalem, "You shall be built," And to the temple, "Your foundation shall be laid."*

Isaiah 45:1 *"Thus says the LORD to* ***His anointed, to Cyrus****, whose right hand I have held - To subdue nations before him and loose the armor of kings,..."*

God stirred the heart of King Cyrus to accomplish His will. Cyrus was moved to make royal decrees: *"Let Jerusalem be rebuilt." "Let the foundations of the Temple be laid."* God moved upon Cyrus and he came into alignment with God's sacred plans and purposes. If God can move the heart of a heathen king to finance and rebuild His Temple and His beloved City, Jerusalem, He can move upon the hearts of kings today to accomplish His will when it comes to His covenant land.

> **Proverbs 21:1** *"The king's heart is in the hand of the LORD, like the rivers of water; He turns it wherever He wishes."*

People of faith, who call upon the Name of the Lord, can agree in prayer that God would move upon the hearts of kings in the earth today to accomplish His will.

In the book of Esther, did God not disturb the sleep of King Ahasuerus and divinely orchestrate that he would read the scrolls in the middle of the night? Since God's people prayed and fasted, God set into motion a succession of events. The king was divinely led to grant Esther the privilege of over-writing Haman's wicked decree that would have destroyed the Jewish people. Esther was granted the privilege of writing a higher decree in the king's name and sealing it with his signet ring.

> **Esther 8:8** *"...write a decree concerning the Jews, as you please, in the king's name, and seal it with the king's signet ring; for whatever is written in the king's name and sealed with the king's signet ring no one can revoke."*

God is the same yesterday, today and forever. He can move in like manner today.

Certain elements of Canada's Foreign policy need to be over written in accordance to God's foreign policy, God's 'one-state solution'.

Prayer has and can move the hand of God in accordance with God's will. With God, all things are possible.

Could it be that God might move upon the government of Canada to change some of the wording of the foreign policy from a 'two-state solution' to a 'one-state solution?'

Could it be that God might move upon the government of Canada to change some of the wording of the foreign policy from *'occupied'* land to *'disputed'* land?

Could it be that Canada might take the lead in aligning its foreign policy with God's Word and other nations might follow?

Our present foreign policy has and will continue to invoke the judgement of God upon our nation. The consequences will be far reaching. Canada's unwavering support for Israel is commendable and unprecedented among all the nations of the world today. However Canada's position on the two-state 'land for peace' *deal* must change. God's plumb-line is immovable. God's covenant land is not to be divided! Jerusalem is not to be divided!

May the policy advisors and decision-makers in Canada's newly appointed government reconsider Canada's foreign policy and come into alignment with the Word of God regarding His covenant land. May the nations of the world review and reconsider their foreign policies regarding God's covenant land and align with the plumb line of God's Word.

As watchmen we continue to sound the shofar, we continue to intercede, we continue to engage. As Canadians, our refrain remains:

God keep our land glorious and free
Oh Canada, we stand on guard for thee.

Stirred by God's Noble Theme!

CHAPTER NINE

WATCHMEN ARISE

Isaiah 62:6,7 *"I have set watchmen on your walls, O Jerusalem; They shall never hold their peace day or night. You who make mention of the Lord, do not keep silent; And give Him no rest till He establishes And till He makes Jerusalem the praise in all the earth."*

I have climbed the ancient watchtower of what is traditionally known as Jeremiah's watchtower at Neot Kedumim, the Biblical Landscape Reserve in Israel, near the remains of an ancient village of Modi'in, the birthplace of the Maccabees.

Make the ascent up the narrow passageway, reach its pinnacle and you will emerge into a most breathtaking panoramic view of the Samarian Hills on one side and the skyline of Tel Aviv, on the Coastal Plain, on the other side.

One can stand on this ancient watch tower and envision what it must have been like to be a watchman in Biblical times. From this vantage point, the watchman would diligently take his stand and peer into the distance. The watchman knew his surroundings. He was intimately acquainted with every detail in the landscape ~ every tree, every bush, the surrounding fields, groves and hills. The watchman would scrutinize as far as his naked eye could see. Anything out of the ordinary would apprehend his attention and awaken his well-honed watchman skills. It was incumbent upon each watchman to be alert and ready to sound the alarm at the sign of impending danger.

THE WATCHMAN

One of the Hebrew words for watchman is *'natsar.'* A person who is commissioned to keep, to watch, to guard, to observe, to protect, to reserve and to preserve. Natsar is a verb. It speaks of active involvement of one who has been posted and commissioned to guard and watch over his master's property, estate or kingdom.

> **Jeremiah, 31:6** *"For there shall be a day when the **watchmen** (notzrim) will cry on Mount Ephraim, 'Arise, and let us go up to Zion, To the LORD our God.'"*

'Notzrim' is the modern Hebrew word for Christians (No·tsri, צְרֵינוּ) (Strong's 5341) and one of two words commonly used to mean 'Christian.' The traditional view is that this word is derived from the Hebrew word for Nazareth *'Nazara'* that was used in ancient times. Nazareth, in turn, may be derived from either na·tsar, נָצַר, meaning *'to watch,'* or from ne·tser, נֵצֶר, meaning branch.

(http://en.wikipedia.org/wiki/Nazarene_(title))

Another Hebrew word for watchman is *'tsaphah.'* (Strong's 6822) Its meaning is to lean forward or to peer into the distance. By implication it means to spy out, to observe, to behold, to wait for and keep watch.

'Shamar' (Strong's 8104) is another Hebrew word for watchman which means to guard, to keep, to watch over, to attend and to defend.

The prophets in the Bible were watchmen in their day, delivering the Word of God and sounding the alarm regarding impending dangers in Israel. They also pronounced warnings to the nations that attempted to thwart God's plans and purposes for His covenant people and His covenant land.

Today, the watchman entrusted with Heaven's commission must exhibit the same due diligence and stand guard over the things assigned to his charge. In like manner, God places watchmen on the walls of Jerusalem. He entrusts His watchmen to *'shamar'* His people, His city and His Kingdom interests.

> **Psalm 127:1** *"Unless the Lord builds the house, they labor in vain who build it; unless* **the Lord guards the city**, *the watchman stays awake in vain."*

God's watchmen are not watching alone nor in vain. They are watching with *'The Chief Watchman'* of Israel, the Lord Himself. He is the Great Shamar, the Great Watchman, the Keeper of Israel!

> **Psalms 121:3-6** *"He will not allow your foot to be moved;* **He who keeps you** *(Israel) will not slumber. Behold,* **He who keeps Israel** *shall neither slumber nor sleep.* **The Lord is your keeper;** *The Lord is your shade at your right hand. The sun shall not strike you by day, nor the moon by night."*

> **Isaiah 62:6,7** *"***I have set watchmen*** on your walls, O Jerusalem; they shall never hold their peace day or night. You who make mention of the Lord, do not keep silent; and give Him no rest till He establishes and till He makes Jerusalem the praise in the earth."*

Watchmen on these walls will not be silent! They will never hold their peace day or night! They cry out to God for His City. They pray for the peace of Jerusalem. They are instructed to give God no rest until all that He has purposed comes to pass, until He establishes and makes Jerusalem 'the' praise in the earth.

Watchmen are diligent to uphold Zion's cause as the existential threat to Israel's very existence increases with every passing day. The shofar must be sounded and nations must heed. These faithful watchmen know the Word of God and stand to defend and uphold the King's interests, the King's treasure.

The Lord Himself anoints and appoints and commissions watchmen to their posts. They must take their stand, be positioned and engaged! It is a high and holy calling to be stationed on the ramparts of the King, representing His interests, guarding His covenant people and His covenant land.

When we sing our national anthem, we are calling on God, the Chief Watchman, to watch guard, protect and keep our land glorious and free. When we sing, *'O Canada, we stand on guard for thee,'* is this not a watchman decree to stand on guard for our nation? If it means sounding the alarm when one sees an imminent danger – so be it!

The alarm is resounding in our land! The trumpet is being blown in Zion! The shofars are resounding in the ancient hills of Judea and yes, in the halls of government in the parliaments in the world.

> **Joel 2:1** *"**Blow the trumpet** in Zion, and **sound an alarm** on My holy mountain! Let all the inhabitants of the land tremble; …for the day of the LORD is coming, for it is at hand:"*

Oh my goodness ~ it's a lot easier or safer to be silent. It's a lot more convenient to be complacent and perhaps more expedient to be politically correct. But once one's heart been stirred by Heaven's ***Noble Theme***, who then can remain silent?

Last year, I spoke at a Christian House of Prayer. At the end of my teaching about *God's heart, Israel and the Nations,* someone asked me, *"What next? What do we do now? Where do we go from here? How do we engage?"* I mentioned that I would love nothing more than to retire in a little cottage on a lake, bake cookies and be with my little grandson reading books with him and playing with him and enjoying a peaceful quiet life. But I quickly added that my heart had been stirred by a ***Noble Theme*** as in Psalm 45:1 and that I could simply not retire nor be silent nor disengaged. I mentioned that in addition to all I was doing, I had so much stirring in my heart that I could write a book. A pastor in the group stood to his feet, I believe he was stirred by the Spirit of God and in a very penetrating fashion pointed his finger directly at me and in a very convicting manner charged, *"Then write the book."* He went on to ask if I knew what the second half of Psalm 45:1 stated. I was all too familiar with the verse:

> **Psalm 45:1** *"My heart is stirred by a Noble Theme as I recite my verses for the king; my tongue is the pen of a skillful writer."* (NIV)

WHY DO THE NATIONS RAGE?

At this present time, the world is in chaos. The nations are raging. The kings of the earth are venting their anger and rage against God. There is an escalation and growing intensity of violence and terror released in almost all the nations of the world today. Hamas, Al Qaida, Hezbolla, the Muslim Brotherhood, Boko Haram and ISIS are spreading their venomous and destructive tentacles in the Middle East, Europe, Asia, the Americas and Africa.

Psalm 2 written by King David thousands of years ago is being played out on the world stage today.

> **Psalm 2:1-6** *"Why do the nations rage, and the people plot a vain thing? The kings of the earth set themselves, and the rulers take counsel together, against the LORD and against His Anointed, saying, Let us break their bonds in pieces and cast away their cords from us. He who sits in the heavens shall laugh; The Lord shall hold them in derision. Then He shall speak to them in His wrath, and distress them in His deep displeasure: 'Yet I have set My King on My holy hill of Zion.'"*

The kings and leaders of the earth are setting themselves up in array against God Almighty and His Anointed One, His Son Jesus Christ! They resolutely set themselves against Him! The root of their rage is spiritual. They see God's loving covenants and commandments as binding cords and bands that they are attempting to break away from in their defiance, rebellion and anger.

God counters their defiance by declaring that their evil alliances, plots and wicked counsel are in vain. They are futile and rendered ineffective. God is sovereign! In quiet confidence, yet in wrath, God trumpets His response! He sits on the circle of the earth and laughs and will have them in derision and confusion. His Anointed is appointed! He has set His King upon Mount Zion, upon His Holy Mountain. It is an established fact in the Spirit. God's Son Jesus, Yeshua, won the victory on the cross. His resurrection power has defeated the enemy on His holy hill of Zion.

Just as there is an escalation of violence and evil, there is a greater escalation of the glory of the Son of God rising in the earth.

> **Isaiah 9:5,6** *"Of the increase of His government and peace, there shall be no end! Upon the throne of David and upon His Kingdom, He has ordered it, to establish it with both judgements and acts of loving-kindness. The zeal of the Lord will perform it."*

We will see the fullness of the manifestation of that crowning moment when the god of this world, Satan, will soon be crushed underfoot by the God of Peace, (Romans 16:20) Yeshua will be enthroned in the New Jerusalem.

> **Psalm 2:10-12** *"Now therefore, be wise, O kings; be instructed, you judges of the earth. Serve the LORD with fear, and rejoice with trembling. Kiss the Son, lest He be angry, and you perish in the way,"*

Watchmen, look through your prophetic lense and capture a glimpse of the final triumph of our Lord Jesus Christ over all His enemies. Simply read Revelation chapters 21 and 22. To that end we labour! This present suffering is not worthy to be compared to the glory that will be revealed and manifest. (Romans 8:18,19) It's going to be worth it all. We can't afford to lay down or drift off to sleep or be apathetic or quiet. With eager expectation we await the glorious and final manifestation of the last two chapters of the Bible. We set our hands to the plough. We run the race set before us. We fight the good fight and war a good warfare.

Watchmen, watch! Intercessors, pray! Take up your posts! Be attentive! Be alert! Stand on guard! Be sober and vigilant! Be engaged! Be strong and courageous! We are not of those who shrink back. Watchmen arise!

PRAY FOR THOSE IN AUTHORITY

> **1 Timothy 2:1,2** *"I urge, then, first of all, that petitions, prayers, intercession and thanksgiving be made for all people—for kings and all those in authority, that we may live peaceful and quiet lives in all godliness and holiness."*

The Biblical imperative and divine exhortation is to pray for kings and those in authority. To what end? That there might be peace in the land and people might experience quiet lives in all godliness and holiness. The effectual fervent prayer of the righteous will avail much.

THE SONS OF ISSACHAR

Mighty men of valour came to David at Hebron to transition the kingdom of Saul to David, according to the Word of the Lord. (1 Chronicles 12:23) A band of mighty men came to David from every tribe of Jacob who were basically described in military terms ~ armed for war, experts in war, they were equipped with buckler and spear and sword and all kinds if instruments of war. They were prepared, trained, equipped and ready for battle with every kind of weapon of war.

They were brave warriors who came to fight with King David, however, one tribe stood out from all the others. They were the men of the children of Issachar who *'understood the times and knew what Israel ought to do.'*

> **1 Chronicles 12:32** *"of the sons of Issachar who had understanding of the times, to know what Israel ought to do..."*

They walked in God-given discernment, understanding and perception. They possessed wisdom to know what to do after they discerned the times and the Word of God. Every situation was weighed on its own merits from Heaven's perspective. They knew the will, the Word and the ways of Jehovah God.

Watchmen today need to be like the men of Issachar discerning and understanding the times and knowing what to do. Jesus said,

> **Matthew 16:3,** *"...You know how to discern the face of the sky, but you cannot discern the signs of the times."*

The watchman must be able to read the signs and discern the times. All things must be judged and weighed from a Biblical perspective. The Bible is the plumb-line! Watchman cannot stand at their posts and be Biblically illiterate!!!

Knowing the heart, the instructions and commands and the kingly standard is imperative! Praying the Word of God and declaring His plans and purposes are necessary. Sounding the alarm when the dangers are imminent are part of the noble call.

When a watchman sees the enemy at the gate attempting to destroy God's people, the apple of His eye, the alarm must be sounded!

When the watchman sees the nations at the gate, or the negotiating table, attempting to carve up Israel's God given inheritance, her covenant land, and attempting to divide the City of Jerusalem, the alarm must be sounded! Giving away Israel's covenant 'land for peace' leaves Israel's borders indefensible. These plans are contrary to God's will. The supportive evidence that links 'land for peace' talks and consequences are astounding. Nations, be aware of what the Word of God says about such matters!

THE WATCHMAN WARNING

Ezekiel 33:7-9 *"So you, son of man: I have made you a watchman for the house of Israel; therefore you shall hear a word from My mouth and warn them for Me. When I say to the wicked, 'O wicked man, you shall surely die!' and you do not speak to warn the wicked from his way, that wicked man shall die in his iniquity; but his blood I will require at your hand. Nevertheless if you warn the wicked to turn from his way, and he does not turn from his way, he shall die in his iniquity; but you have delivered your soul."*

This is the watchman's mandate. The watchman principle was clear. Simply stated, those who heeded the watchman's warning were spared and the watchman would not be held accountable because he released the Word of the Lord in obedience. Conversely, if the watchman did not warn of the impending danger and sound the alarm, he would be held accountable to God. How sobering!

Watchmen, execute your charge. Set the trumpet to your mouth and do not hold back. Do not be silent!

Isaiah 58:1 *"Cry aloud, spare not; lift up your voice like a trumpet..."*

It is a serious matter to fall into the hands of the living God when it comes to dividing the land of Israel. There is a serious warning to be heeded. For Jerusalem and for Zion's sake, we must not be silent. O nations of the earth, hear the word of the Lord! Israel's land is not up for grabs. Israel's land is not to be divided. There will be consequences. The watchmen of the Bible and the watchmen today are sounding the trumpet.

Joel 3:1-3 *"For behold, in those days and at that time, When I bring back the captives of Judah and Jerusalem, I will also gather all nations, And bring them down to the Valley of Jehoshaphat; And **I will enter into judgment with them** there on account of My people, My heritage Israel, **Whom they have scattered among the nations; They have also divided up My land. They have cast lots for My people.**"*

HOW LONG?

How long do the watchmen stand on the walls? (Isaiah 62:6a)

How long should they remain silent? (Isaiah 62:6b)

How long should they give themselves and God no rest? (Isaiah 62:7a)

Until... God makes Jerusalem the praise in all the earth! (Isaiah 62:7b)

Until... we see the fulfilment and glorious manifestation of the last two chapters of the Bible. (Revelation 21 & 22)

Until... we see the Holy City, the New Jerusalem, coming down out of Heaven from God, prepared as a bride beautifully dressed for her husband. (Revelation 21:2)

Until... the tabernacle of God is with men, and He will dwell with them, and they shall be His people. God Himself will be with them and be their God. (Revelation 21:3)

Until... He wipes away every tear from their eyes! (Revelation 21:4a)

Until... there will be no more death, nor crying, nor mourning, nor pain, for the old order of things has passed away! (Revelation 21:4b)

Until... a great multitude that no one could count from every nation, tribe, people, and language will stand before the throne and in front of the Lamb singing, *"Amen! Praise and glory and wisdom and thanks and honor and power and strength be to our God forever and ever. Amen! Holy! Holy! Holy! is the Lord God Almighty Who was and is and is to come! Worthy is the Lamb who was slain."* (Revelation 7, 9, 11; 4:8; 5:12)

Until... the kingdoms of this world have become the Kingdom of our God and His Christ and He will reign forever and ever! HalleluYAH! (Revelation 11:15b)

Until... at the name of Jesus every knee should bow, of those in heaven, and of those on earth, and of those under the earth. (Philippians 2:10)

Until... the Lord rebuilds Zion and appears in His glory! (Psalm 102:16)

Psalm 102:12-16 *"But you, LORD, sit enthroned forever; your renown endures through all generations. You will arise and have compassion on Zion, for it is time to show favor to her; the appointed time has come. For her stones are dear to your servants; her very dust moves them to pity. The nations will fear the name of the LORD, all the kings of the earth will revere your glory. For the LORD will rebuild Zion and appear in his glory."* (NIV)

Isaiah 62:1 *"For Zion's sake I will not keep silent, for Jerusalem's sake I will not remain quiet, til her vindication shines out like the dawn, her salvation like a blazing torch."* (NIV)

For Zion's sake, we the watchmen will not be silent nor hold our peace.

Watchmen Arise

> Watchmen, I call you, it's time to arise!
> Heed the voice of My Spirit and you will be wise.
> For now is the time for you to awake.
> You must not be silent for Zion's sake!
>
> An Issachar anointing I will give to you,
> Understanding the times, knowing what you should do.
> The hour is urgent, do not delay,
> For now is the time and this is the day!
>
> Blow the trumpet in Zion and sound the alarm!
> For many the foe who would do Israel harm.
> The Hamans, the Hitlers, the Hamas of this day.
> Would destroy My people and wipe them away.
>
> Hezbollah, Al Qaida, the advancing of ISIS
> Thrusting the world into chaos and crisis.
> They'll try to push Israel right off the map,
> But I call you this day to stand in the gap!
>
> The nations want also to divide up My land,
> Invoking the judgements that come from My Hand.
>
> I'm commissioning you watchmen in a powerful way.
> Now is the time to stand in the fray!
> Mighty are those who obey My command
> And engage in the battle and take up their stand.
>
> This is the day of strategic alignments,
> I'm positioning you for My end time assignments.
> I call you as watchmen to stand on the wall.
> My grace is sufficient when you answer the call.
>
> Position yourselves for I am also appointing.
> A corporate end time Esther anointing.
> To take up My scepter and walk through My land!
> Obey My instructions and keep My command!

Stand firm in your calling and take up your sword,
The most powerful weapon, the Word of the Lord!
Proclaim and decree and begin to declare.
Speak what I decree and proclaim everywhere.
For My Word will prosper, each prophecy told,
Proclaim with authority! Be very bold!

Do not be distracted. Do not be deterred.
Fix your eyes upon Me and give heed to My Word.
For what I have purposed shall never fail.
And the gates of the enemy shall never prevail.

Don't be discouraged and don't ever fear,
For My presence is with you, I'll always be near.
As you fall into rank and each take your place.
Always remember to seek My Face.

Consumed with a holy and passionate zeal,
I'm sending you out to do all I reveal.
So pass through the gates and prepare the way.
Remove all the stones and build a highway.
I'll raise up a banner for the nations through you.
And you'll be amazed at all I will do.

Watchmen, I call you, it's time to arise!
Heed the voice of My Spirit and you will be wise!
One more thing I must tell you, lest I be remiss,
***"You were brought to My Kingdom
For a Time Such As This!***

Whatever God says, we will do! Wherever He leads, we will go! For Zion's sake we will not keep silent. For Jerusalem's sake we will not remain quiet. May the strong winds of Heaven blow and move upon the hearts of more and more watchmen whose voices rise together to sound the alarm and blow the shofar in the nations of the world regarding God's covenant land and His covenant people because they have been ~ ***Stirred by God's Noble Theme!***

CHAPTER TEN

STIRRED BY A NOBLE THEME

Psalm 45:1 *"My heart is stirred by a Noble Theme."* (NIV)

The writer of the book of Ecclesiastes concluded his great work with a profound entreaty,

Ecclesiastes 12:13 *"Now all has been heard; here is the conclusion of the matter: Fear God and keep his commandments, for this is the duty of all mankind."* (NIV)

Stirred by a Noble Theme concludes in like manner. The Biblical framework has been set. The facts have been presented. The dots have been connected. Now that all has been heard, here is the conclusion of the matter: Honor God! Revere Him! Align with His heart and purposes for Israel and the nations. Keep His commands and divine imperatives. Embrace His *Noble Theme*!

God's loving plans for Israel and the Nations is *His Noble Theme*!

He who has an ear let him hear what the Spirit of the God of Israel is saying today.

At a particular time in Israel's history, Moses arose and asked the nation this question,

Exodus 32:26 *"Whoever is on the LORD's side - come to me!"*

Moses drew a line, so to speak. He expected a response. All those whose hearts had been stirred by the Lord came and stood with Moses.

At another time in Israel's history, Joshua, Moses' successor, arose and boldly stated,

> **Joshua 24:14,15** *"Now therefore, fear the LORD, serve Him in sincerity and in truth, ... Serve the LORD! ...Choose for yourselves this day whom you will serve, ...But as for me and my house, we will serve the LORD."*

All those whose hearts had been stirred stood with Joshua and confessed,

> **Joshua 24:24** *"And the people said to Joshua, "The LORD our God we will serve, and His voice we will obey!"*

At another time in Israel's history, the prophet Elijah summoned the people from all over Israel along with 450 prophets of Baal and 400 prophets of Asherah. He went before the people and said,

> **1 Kings 18:21** *"How long will you falter between two opinions? If the LORD is God, follow Him; but if Baal, follow him."*

The Lord answered by fire and all the people whose hearts had been stirred said, *"The Lord – He is God! The Lord – He is God!"*

Today, individuals and nations are being weighed in the balance. On numerous issues, choices must be made. There is no middle ground. There is no sitting on the fence. There is no room for ambiguity. Choose, one must. Choosing wisely is essential. Ultimately, aligning with or opposing *God's Noble Theme* can be a matter of life or death.

The God of Abraham, Isaac and Jacob began his noble work on the earth in Eden and will complete all things according to His stated promises and prophecies in the fullness of time.

Everything that is honorable, good, upright, virtuous, righteous, decent and praiseworthy are woven into the fabric of God's *Noble Theme*.

God's plans and purposes for His covenant people are *Noble*!

God's plans and purposes for His covenant land are *Noble*!

God's plan of redemption and salvation for mankind through His Son, Yeshua the Messiah, is the most superlative and *Noble Theme* from Genesis to Revelation.

The last two chapters of the Bible vividly and clearly display the crowning victory and beauty of God's *Noble Theme*.

THY WORD IS TRUTH

As the saying goes, *"Truth is truth whether accepted or not."*

To reject God's truth or stand on the opposite side of God's truth can be a perilous choice.

The Apostle John clearly stated in 1 John chapter 4 that the spirit of anti-Messiah would come in the last days. Though the nature and spirit of anti-Christ has been prevalent in every generation, it will be manifest in greater measure in the last days. The meaning of the word *'anti'* means *'instead of'* or someone who is *'against'* or *'opposite.'*

Anti-Christ, anti-Messiah or anti 'the Anointed One,' all mean one and the same thing. Any person opposing the Word, the will, the Messiah, the gospel, Israel, Zion, the Jewish people or anything good, noble, righteous, decent, just, pure, honest and praiseworthy is standing against the God of Israel. To stand on the opposite side and oppose Adonai, is to stand on the side of cursing God. One of the meanings of the Hebrew word *'to curse'* is *'qalal'* which means to stand on the opposite side or to oppose.

The great and deceptive question was first posed in the Garden of Eden. Doubt was cast upon the Word of God when the serpent said, *"Has God indeed said, 'You shall not eat of every tree of the garden'?"* (Genesis 3:1) Adam and Eve stood on the other side that day and fell for the lie. They doubted God and then opposed the Word of God. Mankind has suffered ever since. Today, in this dispensation of grace, in the multitude of God's mercies, mankind is given the choice of accepting or rejecting truth. God's Word is truth!

John 17:17 *"Sanctify them by Your truth. Your word is truth."*

John 14:6 *"Jesus said to him, "I am the way, the **truth**, and the life. No one comes to the Father except through Me."*

Whether looking at dividing the land of Israel, scattering the people of Israel, cursing or blessing the Jewish people or accepting the Jewish Messiah, choices must be made.

Moses asked, *"Who is on the Lord's side?"*

Joshua stated, *"Choose today whom you will serve!"*

Elijah implored, *"How long will you falter between two opinions?"*

Ecclesiastes 12:13 *"Now all has been heard; here is the conclusion of the matter: Fear God and keep his commandments, for this is the duty of all mankind."* (NIV)

Now is the time to embrace God's heart and align with His loving plans and purposes for Israel and the nations.

Now is the time to be totally and completely ~ ***Stirred by God's Noble Theme!***

EPILOGUE

THE NEW JERUSALEM

Joel stood at the threshold of eternity. Before him the New Jerusalem was descending from Heaven, from God, prepared like a bride adorned for her husband. [1] That which he saw thousands of years ago in the heavenly vision, inside the burning and passionate heart of God, was now a blazing reality. God's dream, ***God's Noble Theme***, was now vibrant and visible. The manifestation of the glory of God was dazzling in brilliance. The New Jerusalem [2] was now 'the' praise of all the earth. [3] The City God loved was made new and filled with an innumerable company from every nation and tribe and people and language. [4] God's heart, Israel and the nations were together. His people now filled His City. They were a people redeemed and purchased by the blood of the Lamb Who was slain before the foundation of the world. [5] Grafted into God's Abrahamic covenant, through God's Son, Yeshua, [6] they came.

The kingdoms of the world became the Kingdom of our Lord and of His Messiah, Yeshua, and He now reigns forever and ever! [7] Hallelu~YAH!

Joel, felt once again, that which stirred in the heart of God from eternity past. The City whose Builder and Maker was God [8] now stood before Him in indescribable beauty with walls of jasper, gates of pearl, foundations adorned with every precious stone, with streets made of pure gold, like translucent glass. [9]

Kings of the earth conspired against the Holy One and His Anointed One. [10] Empires battled unabated. Wars waged and raged relentlessly. Hordes of hell paraded in ceaseless procession. Adversaries unyielding in pursuit attempted to destroy Israel, divide and seize God's covenant land and His beloved and chosen City, Jerusalem. However, the gates of Hell did not prevail! [11]

Though schemes of devils and demons, callous and cruel caliphates, heinous horrors of the Holocaust, terrors of pogroms, pernicious evils of inquisitions and twisted ideologies of man, attempted to abort God's redemptive plan of salvation, the Son of God triumphed victoriously on the cross. Having disarmed principalities and powers, He made a public spectacle of them, triumphing over them in it. [12]

Every enemy was vanquished. Death was destroyed forever! Yes, death was swallowed up in victory! Death had lost its sting.[13] Suffering and sorrow, tears and mourning, now stood as faint shadows in the dim and distant past. Nations would never lift up sword against nation again, neither would they learn of war any more. [14]

God's Noble Theme marched forward in time and now the culmination and crescendo of His greatest refrain reached its crowning moment! What Joel gazed upon that day was the glorious coronation, the radiant splendour and amazing manifestation of all that God desired and planned and purposed from eternity past. This was the perfection and expression of that which was birthed in the Holy heart of the Ancient of Days!

God's Son, Faithful and True, [15] the Word of God, [16] was now enthroned forever and ever as King of kings and Lord of lords! [17]

Once again, Joel stood in silence. What he had prophesied and proclaimed, what he envisioned and saw by faith, was now overwhelming him. This was the magnificent and majestic outworking of God's dream, ***God's Noble Theme.***

No light and momentary affliction[18] nor any of the cheap substitutes, the fleeting pleasures, the deceitfulness of riches, the pride of life, the worldly ambitions nor the vain attractions contrived and manufactured by man, were worthy to be compared to the blazing glory that was now on display.

What Joel beheld was unbelievably believable and incredibly credible! Joel burst into acclamations of jubilant praise to his God and thanked Him that thousands of years earlier, by faith, he saw, he believed, he received and he delivered the Word of God and lived for the dream, **God's Noble Theme!** Like Abraham, he too had been looking for the City whose Builder and Maker and Architect was God!

The voice of God penetrated Joel's being. He was arrested. Heaven's voice echoed throughout the Great City and resonated in the hearing of His ears, *"What do you see? Joel, what do you see?"*

His response,

> *I see Your heart.*
> *I see Your dream.*
> *I see Your City.*
> *Your Noble Theme!*
>
> *I see Your splendour,*
> *A glorious thing!*
> *I see my Saviour,*
> *Yeshua, My King!*
>
> *I see Your people,*
> *Saved by Your grace!*
> *The highest reward…*
> *I see Your face!*
>
> *I see Jerusalem,*
> *All things You esteem.*
> *I'll stand forever,*
> *Beholding Your Dream!*
> *I'm stirred forever,*
> *By **Your Noble Theme!***

Softly, in the serenity of that celestial moment, they came! They came from every tribe and tongue and language and race. They came! They continued to come, a vast number as far as the eye could see. They stood with Him, an innumerable company, a celestial family, raptured by the eternal embrace of the God they loved and lived for. They came singing and praising their God whom they adored. Nothing could ever quench the flame of this love! [19] And with them, the crowning glory, KING YESHUA, Son of God, The Lamb of God who took away the sin of the world. The Lamb of God who by His blood purchased His Bride. [20] Selah!

Joel heard the song of his God, its melody forever swirling in the mansions of eternity. It was Heaven's refrain,

> *No greater joy, no greater elation,*
> *My family now here from every nation.*
>
> *The battle is over! My Son with His Bride,*
> *Whom He bought with His blood, now stands at His side.*
>
> *Behold with your eyes, this was always my dream,*
> *Eternally burning as* ***My Noble Theme!***

"Even so, Come, Lord Jesus"
Revelation 22:20
Bo, Yeshua (Hebrew)

1) Revelation 21:2
2) Revelation 21:2
3) Isaiah 62:7
4) Revelation 7:9
5) Revelation 13:8
6) Romans 11:17
7) Revelation 11:15
8) Hebrews 11:10
9) Revelation 21:18-21
10) Psalm 2:1,2
11) Matthew 16:18
12) Colossians 2:15
13) 1 Corinthians 15:54,55
14) Isaiah 2:4
15) Revelation 19:11
16) John 1:1
17) Revelation 19:16
18) 2 Corinthians 4:17
19) Song of Songs 8:7
20) 1 Corinthians 6:20

About the Book

Writing a book about the heart, plans and purposes of God is a weighty and serious undertaking. It is my prayer that the reader's gaze would turn heavenward and be **Stirred by God's Noble Theme**.

I felt compelled by the God of Israel, to write **Stirred by a Noble Theme**. I sensed an invitation from God Himself to come to His beloved City Jerusalem for one entire month to sit alone with Him, to pour through the scriptures and capture His heart and His passion for Israel and the nations. There was an overwhelming sense of needing to be in His covenant land, in His covenant City, among His covenant people. It was my 30th trip to Israel. I sat in the secret place of the Most High, under the shadow of El Shaddai. I walked the streets of Jerusalem and the hills and valleys surrounding Mount Moriah, the Temple Mount. I sat for hours at the Western Wall listening, meditating, observing and absorbing the sounds and catching the heartbeat of the most holy place on earth, the place of God's throne, the place of His heart, the place God calls His favorite place. I was immersed in God's heart and began to write **His Noble Theme**. I embarked on an amazing journey that unfolded throughout the writing of this book.

> **Psalm 39:3** *"My heart grew hot within me. While I meditated, the fire burned; then I spoke with my tongue:"* (NIV) *...and began to write.*

Habakkuk 2:1,2 *"I will stand my watch and set myself on the rampart, and watch to see what He will say to me,…write the vision and make it plain on tablets, that he may run who reads it."*

The final chapters of the book were written in Ottawa, Canada in the prayer chapel on Parliament Hill overlooking the Peace Tower and the Prime Minister's official office. I began writing in Israel's capital city and ended in Canada's capital city.

I am profoundly grateful to God for this opportunity to have been invited to walk this path and scribe what I believe He led me to write. I pray that many hearts, lives, governments and nations will be touched, inspired, challenged, changed and transformed by *God's Noble Theme*.

My heart has been eternally stirred by God's Noble Theme

Annie Elliott